I0169012

The Last Stress-busting Book You'll Ever Need
Robert Chute BJ (HONS) RMT

Published by Ex Parte Press
Copyright © 2016
All rights reserved.
ISBN 978-1-927607-44-2

Please address inquiries to expartepress@gmail.com

To my fellow massage therapists, Brenda Beattie, Victor Morin and Jeff Hansen, thank you for all your encouragement and help in the preparation of this book.

Heaps of gratitude to Dr. Janice Kurita, Dr. Rod Overton, Russell Sawatsky, and Mark Victor Young
for your invaluable editorial assistance.

To Dr. Leslie Young editor of *Massage & Bodywork*,
thanks for getting me on the road to writing this book years ago.

To my little sister, Sher Kruse, thanks for inspiring me to tackle this project now.

No one who does well does it alone.

Table of Contents

The Obligatory Disclaimer

My goal is to provide you with results-oriented suggestions and practical solutions to become your best self (and stressing less along the way). Welcome to *Do The Thing!* You're about to get a much better handle on the management of stress, pain, time and energy. (Life, in other words.)

You will read observations about techniques I've found useful over the years based on study, research and experience. Individual reactions vary. This book is not meant to supplant any diagnosis, treatment or medical advice. I can't control how your body and mind will react to every stimulus. Therefore, please treat this book as a buffet of ideas to explore. Take what you can use personally and safely. Leave the rest. Nobody sane and healthy eats every item at the buffet.

My journey along the stress-busting path started early. I was a stressed-out child barreling into an anxious adulthood. An early interest in self-defense took me from martial arts class and into meditation. I read everything I could about the human potential movement. That subculture faded. However, the human potential movement has been reborn in the last decade, largely due to technology. We have plenty of tech that causes us more stress and we have more technology to help us deal with that stress.

The goals of the sixties and seventies have reemerged amid more individual and technologically oriented pursuits: Biohacking, transhumanism, obsessive digital journaling and measurement of biological markers and so on. This is not a book about biohacking. You'll find my suggestions are more accessible to everyone. Most suggestions I'll give you will be low tech, inexpensive and, as you might have guessed from the title, readily doable.

Trained first in journalism and philosophy, I researched these subjects deeply and worked to apply the best suggestions to my life. As a manual therapist, I use these tools for myself and, where appropriate, for my clients. In this book, you'll find tips, tricks and things to think about that will help you manage your time and energy while reducing stress and pain.

Our lives are time and energy. I don't mean that in a hippie-dippy woo-woo mystical way. The information you'll get here is grounded in reality and practice. *Do the Thing!* focuses on life management strategies because when we talk about stress management, it's really all about the optimal use of our time and energy.

I have suffered anxiety and depression but that seems to be behind me now. I'm more organized and suffer less stress than I used to. I hope the ideas presented here will help you as much as they have helped me.

If you exhibit signs of depression or anxiety detailed in the chapter *Caution. Proceed Carefully,* please pick up the phone, get medical help and support. When in doubt, please seek the counsel of your doctor. No book can replace proper medical care so, please, do take care of yourself. Together we will find equilibrium.

Do the things that seem useful and enjoy this book.

Author's Note

You're stressed so I'm going to dispense with an elaborate introduction. There are tons of books on stress management so thank you for choosing this one. I'll just tell you quickly how this book can help you manage or reduce your stressors.

In my research I found that many books in this genre do a lot of throat-clearing before they get to the meat of the issues. Worse, some authors try to scare readers with long lists of the dire consequences* if you don't manage the stresses of living well. You already bought this book! You're interested in stress management. We'll skip the filler and I won't make your stress worse by trying to scare you into a new life.

My mission is to decrease your stress. Much stress relief advice boils down to, "Get your shit together and you'll feel stress." You're not an idiot. You knew that much already. I can't say that adage is wrong, exactly, but it is simplistic. The question is, "*How* do I get my shit together?" I can help with that. If you're new to stress management, you'll find my tactics easy to implement. Enjoyable things that are easy to do continue to get done. If you are already familiar with ways to manage your stress, you'll find helpful angles on old ideas here.

Most people read books in a linear fashion, cover to cover. However, if you're the sort who likes to jump around a book packed with tips, I'd like to help you find what you're looking for quickly.

Section I delves into stress management.

Section II is about time management.

Section III discusses pain management.

Section IV will help you manage your energy.

With so many tips stuffed into this tome, I felt I had to organize the content into general categories for your ease and reading comfort. However, as you'll soon see, stress, time and energy are interrelated and often inseparable factors that influence your effectiveness and happiness. If you're in pain, too, that will be a major factor you'll have to add to your stress management strategies. As always, take what you can safely implement. The rest is for someone else. However, I encourage you to think holistically. If you focus on only one component of stress management or fail to address causes, you will not receive the full benefit. I want you to be happy you bought this book.

So much for the appetizer. Let the feast begin!

* If you really can't resist finding out about all those dire health consequences (or find fear motivating) that scary list of negative health consequences is easy to find. Take a quick peek at a search engine if you must. Lists of negative consequences tend to have a short-term effect at best and don't help you manage stress. I'll accentuate the positive: you'll soon discover a plethora of tips and tricks to live easier, breezier and well, minus the scare tactics.

SECTION I

STRESS MANAGEMENT

This is for You

You can relax every day. Yes, you really can. Welcome to your new self-care DIY project.

Relaxation is not merely a fuel pump you can drive up to, get your fill and move on until you burn it off. It's achievable every day and, largely, you can do it yourself. As your relaxation consultant, I'm here to help you get optimal, mentally and physically. Every day, I tell my clients the same thing: look for opportunities to achieve relaxation for more than just an hour or two a month. We're all too busy, overstimulated and overstressed. I'm here to help provide solutions that won't increase your bills and spread the stress around. Most suggestions in this book are cheap or free.

Relaxation is your responsibility. It makes you happier, more effective and easier to get along with. Stressed people are irritable. Whatever the cause of your stress, pushing people away, tightening your muscles, despairing or getting angry probably will not help you in getting past life's obstacles.

Sometimes someone will rush into my office late and harried. They are desperate to relax but they don't really know how. As soon as their session is done, mentally, they're winding up again. These are overcommitted people whose lives are not under their control. Though I have helped therapeutically, I haven't quite reached them yet.

Let's go explore stress reduction and relaxation strategies so everyone can be reached.

Do the relaxing thing.

The First Rule of Stress Management

The first rule of stress management is do not worry about what you can't control.

There! Most of your worries are already eliminated. I'll help you figure out how to worry less, too. Let's spend the rest of this guide dealing with what stress is left over.*

*Hint:
This book can't help you if you don't read it.
Turn off and turn away from your distractions and do the reading thing.

Check In

If one is the least and ten is the worst, what number would you put on your stress between one and ten? Answer the first number that comes to mind.

Let's take a moment to check in with your current state, just to see how awareness can turn things around. Put the index and middle fingertips of your left hand over the pulse at your right wrist. Notice the beat of your heart. Note your heart rate. How many beats per minute are you clocking? Got a number?

Now, just for a moment, close your eyes and take a deep breath. Repeat a few deep breaths, nice and slow. Shrug your shoulders up toward your ears and feel the muscles contract before allowing them to relax. Do it again, and this time, as you exhale, allow your shoulders to drop.

Now imagine there is a string at your sternum pulling straight up, as you take another deep abdominal breath and let it out slowly. Look for tension. Do you find any discomfort in your feet? Any tension in your back? Your legs? Wherever you find tension, let it go, if you can. Often, simply becoming aware of your muscular tension is the beginning of releasing it.

One last time, take a deep breath and, as you exhale, smile.

The aim of this exercise is simply to draw awareness to the muscular tension you were feeling unconsciously. I suggest you check in on your level of stress throughout the day for a while, getting into the habit of higher awareness.

Time to check in again.

What number would you put on your stress between one and ten now? Answer the first number that comes to mind.

Check your pulse again. Is it slower?

Were you surprised at how much tension you found?

Has the muscular tension lessened at least a little now that you've allowed yourself to become aware of it?

Repeat this awareness exercise whenever you are uncomfortable. Discomfort is the cue to get into the habit of higher awareness and less stress.

Do the awareness thing.

Awareness Exercise.

Please write your answer to the following questions:

On a scale of one to ten, one being mild and ten severe, what number would you put on your pain?

On a scale of one to ten, one being mild and ten severe, what number would you put on your stress?

On a scale of one to ten, one being very little and ten being vibrant, what number would you put on your energy?

PAIN

STRESS

ENERGY

Did you do the rating thing? Good. Now turn the page to understand the crucial connections among these three key components and what it means for your stress management strategy.

Pain, Energy, Stress

You recorded the pain, stress and energy scores, right?

Understand that these numbers are subjective. That's okay. Listen to your body and acknowledge that you feel what you feel. These numbers are useful as a baseline.

Record your pain, stress and energy numbers now if you haven't already. After a month of using the anti-stress tactics in this book, check in to see how you've improved, by how much and in which areas. You'll be pleasantly surprised at your progress. Even if you try just a few of these stress management tactics, expect improvement.

You probably have more than one book on your bookshelf about dealing with stress. You might have a bunch more on weight loss, organization and healthy living cookbooks. Most of them go unread or unused. So, let's find the proof in the pudding. If you give my strategies an honest shot, what are your numbers? Find the proof in the pudding below.

PUDDIN' PROOF:

Today's date:

Pain score:
Stress score:
Energy score:

At one week:

Pain score:
Stress score:
Energy score:

One month later:

Pain score:
Stress score:

Energy score:

Three months later:

Pain score:
Stress score:
Energy score:

Six months:

Pain score:
Stress score:
Energy score:

One year:

Pain score:
Stress score:
Energy score:

To make sure you stay on top of pain, stress and energy scores and actually follow through, I suggest you set up a spreadsheet in Google Docs and track your ups and downs regularly. If you take note of the score every Sunday (after church or after *The Walking Dead*, whatever cue works for you) your compliance will be much higher.

Do the tracking thing.

Now, on to the crucial bit. Let's do some pattern recognition! Turn the page and let's put these numbers to greater use.

The Ups and Downs of Pain, Stress and Energy

There's a relationship among these variables: pain, stress and energy.

When pain goes up, energy goes down.

When energy is high, stress tends to go down (unless you need that energy to run from a burning house.)

When pain goes down, stress goes down.

Simple stuff, right? However, you should also be aware that when stress is high, you become more pain-sensitive. Muscles tighten. Keep muscles tight requires energy. Energy steadily depletes.

I don't mention this as a scare tactic, but to point out that much of stress management is actually aiming at the wrong target. Successful stress management tactics are actually about energy management. When you relax the body, using yoga, for instance, your mind will let go of its mental tension. One affects the other.

A little clever life hacking makes everything go smoothly. Life hackers know that they make better decisions when their energy is high. They tend to make big decisions when their energy is peaking. They use routines that limit their choices for less important matters (e.g. What am I going to wear in the morning? What's for breakfast?)

Successful life hackers manage energy. That's what you're going to do, too.

Turn the page to dig into doing the energy management thing!

Stress Management is Life Management

Money is not time. Time is life. Spend carefully.

Do the prudent thing.

Eustress Versus Distress

Contrary to what many people believe, *not* all stress is bad.

Hans Selye identified positive stress in the 1970s. He called it eustress.

Eustress is stress that spurred people to meet challenges. Eustress is a positive force in our lives.

Think of eustress as engaging a healthy sense of competition. Competing to try harder in a sport or to meet a goal is useful and energizing. (Of course, if you're too competitive, you're that person who is never happy with second place, gloats and becomes a pariah to all your former friends.) Perspective and balance will guide you.

Selye had another name for negative stress: distress. Distress is identified as stress that is unresolved.

Unresolved stress is very common. This book is full of suggestions to help you give up your membership in the Chronically Distressed Club.

Once upon a time, a gentleman told me he had the answer to all stress. I leaned in, eager to hear the secret. He said, to free himself from stress, all he had to do was get done what needed to be done.

I was disappointed in his answer. He was a health professional who should have known better. As anyone who has a job, is unemployed, has children or is childless will tell you, all that stuff that needs to get done? It never really gets done. There is no end to the to-do list.

For most people living a modern life, his so-called strategy was kind of like saying, I'll come to bed when I finish Twitter or Instagram. Twitter and Instagram are never done.

Right about now, someone reading this will be thinking, but this is the best time to be alive! Don't you think cave people had real stress? Running around trying to avoid getting eaten by a saber tooth tiger would be real stress! What are you whiners talking about?

**On the next page, read about
doing the natural thing.**

Flight, Flee or Freeze?

Think you've got it hard? You probably do! I won't tell you that you don't have a stress problem or try to minimize your worries. Stress, its effects and costs, are real. However, consider this: Despite its simplicity, primitive peoples often did indeed live very challenging lives. Depending how far you want to go back, you can identify many stressors.

When ancient people encountered stress — getting chased by something that wanted to eat them, for instance — there were three choices:

Fight.

Flight.

Freeze.

Most people have heard of the fight or flight reflex. If you corner a deer and give it nowhere to run, it will start beating the crap out of you with its sharp little hooves.

The advantage of fight or flight is that these reactions are finite. As the Stranger says in *The Big Lebowski*, "Some days you eat the bear and some days the bear eats you."

Eating or eaten, the stressor is resolved in short order. Ancient people often escaped stress by going to early graves. With modern stress, fight or flight is rarely an option. Stressors can go unresolved, often indefinitely. That's the sort of thing that makes us freeze.

The freeze reflex occurs when stress is high but you can't flee or fight. Emotional and decision-making pathways go into paralysis. Learned helplessness may not be far behind if you don't deal with stress more effectively.

Suppose for a moment that you get sued or the tax department comes knocking about an audit. It will prey on your mind. Lawyers or accountants will have to be called. Even if you've done nothing wrong and you're confident the issue will be successfully resolved, it will take time. This sort of thing can devolve into a massive energy suck. You can't go beat up your auditor and you can't run away. While you wait, you may freeze. That's understandable but you do have options.

Now imagine that you have a job where you're dealing with a rude and unreasonable boss. If you fight, you lose the job you need and you go to jail. If you flee, where is the money going to come from so you can live a life free and easy on a tropical beach? That leaves you in paralysis, unable to act and disempowered. Freezing certainly feels like it makes sense, doesn't it?

Don't be the bear who eats others alive.
Don't be a deer in headlights.
Do the human thing.

What have we learned so far?

Some of the easiest stress-busting strategies allow you to resolve something in short order. Remember? According to Selye, distress is *unresolved* stress.

When people tell me they have a lot on their plates and they wish they could bust a bunch of stress quick, I ask, "Well, what can you resolve quickly?"

The answer could be the simple breathing and awareness exercise we started with in Check in #1.

Making your bed or scrubbing the tub may be a quick ticket to that feeling of accomplishment you crave. It may help you to ease your stress by choosing a project you can get done on a short deadline. A little hit of the happy hormone dopamine gets released when we accomplish something.

We have to be careful about how and when we get that feel good dopamine release. Vegging out and losing yourself to video games and social media does have its place. When you are low on energy and you've done all you planned for the day to advance your goals, why not?

It is not my goal to turn you into a life-hacking, life-hating robot who is accomplished, successful and run into the ground. If your work efficiency is at 100%, screaming, crying and a nervous breakdown are rarely far behind. Be a happy and effective human, not a sad robot.

**To bust stress,
do the quickly resolved thing.**

What's Your Button?

My favorite stress study of all time forced subjects to do math under duress. I hate math, so I could relate.

Here's the set up:

Take the victims you're experimenting upon and stick them in a room with a chair and a desk.

On the desk, they'll find several sheets of math problems. Play some loud, obnoxious music in the background. Make it loud enough that it's actually in the foreground.

Stressful, right? Now for the fun stuff.

Take whatever measurements you like (blood cortisol, fast respiration, heartbeat, sweat, tears, whatever). The subject's stress is going to be high.

Second scenario:

Give the subjects a button on the desk. The button, they are told, will decrease the volume of the music blasting behind his or her head. If they need it, they can push it and solve the problems in greater peace and quiet.

No surprise:

In the second group, all the measures of stress will be lower.

Conclusion:

Establishing more control over the variables of your life will lower your stress.

But there *is* a surprise.

With the second group, people who did not push the volume button *still* exhibited lower stress measures!

In other words, not only will establishing more control over the variables of your life lower your stress, even the *illusion* of control lowers stress.

Despite the language used in this fascinating study, please note that *control* isn't the most helpful word. We do not control our lives. We manage our time and energy. That attitude makes a huge difference.

To help you bust stress, we will need to establish guidelines that will help you manage your life variables. Accept that there are things you cannot control. You can't control how tall you are or aren't. There are genetic variables and age-related factors to disease that are beyond our power to assert control.

No reasonable person expects you to control everything. We're all doing the best we can with the resources we have. This guide will increase the number of resources at your disposal. However, please don't put unreasonable pressure on yourself. Be more kind and compassionate to yourself than that.

Remember the very first tip in this book?
Don't worry about what you can't control.

Tactics are short-term actions. Strategies are long-term. There is some nuance we must cover before getting into the nitty gritty.

We'll find the buttons to turn down your stress. First, please turn the page for an important message.

Do the nuanced thing.

Caution. Proceed Carefully.

When stress is severe, people can get stuck.
If you consistently rate your stress and pain as high and your energy stays low, consult health professionals.

How do you know if you're suffering depression or anxiety?

Are you suffering guilt, debilitating loneliness or have you become so down that you withdraw? Do you find that activities you used to enjoy no longer bring you pleasure? Are you finding it hard to get out of bed? Are you sleeping more than usual? Have you missed work? Are you losing sleep or self-medicating?

You might be depressed or anxious. (You can be both at the same time.) **If in doubt, you need more help than a guide to stress management can give. Please seek out medical assistance.**

If you have a plan to hurt yourself or others, get to an Emergency Room immediately. Don't hurt yourself or anyone else. That's not a solution. That's another problem. Call for help. Go to Suicide.org. They have suicide prevention hotlines listed worldwide. Call.

Unfortunately, stress, anxiety and mental illness are terribly stigmatized in our society. I think that's changing, but I don't think it's changing fast enough. People generally understand that if you have diabetes, you're going to need to manage the problem with strict diet, exercise and probably insulin. However, if the problem is stress or depression, they expect you to "tough it out," "suck it up," or "walk it off."

Show compassion to yourself and others. Do not contribute to the stigma. Depression, like any other disease, is not easily dismissed.

Do the generous thing.
Get and give help.

Rinse & Repeat

Every suggestion you implement must be repeated. Repetition makes the solutions in this book a reality. Repeat all solutions as necessary.

Expect this pattern:

Mindset.

Action.

Adjust.

Enjoy.

Repeat.

**To make healthier choices a habit,
do the good things regularly.**

Mindset

Everything you do has an opportunity cost. Do not work hard at stuff that doesn't matter.

Remember how I mentioned that when we talk about stress management, it's very much about energy management? Here's where you get traction with stress busting. Evaluate what you are paying in time and ask yourself: does this help me toward my long-term goals? Or is this busywork?

Busywork is everywhere. When your kids get 87 math questions that take hours and they already understand the concept after 15 equations? That's busywork. More homework doesn't help them. It just sucks time.

Busywork does not build character. It doesn't do good in the world. It's a waste of time. That's all it is. Avoid getting sucked into it.

Work that is not work for its own sake carries you toward your goals. Useful work has measurable positive outcomes.

Do the measuring thing.

The Tyranny of the Protestant Work Ethic

Everybody serves someone. Pretty much everyone does some kind of work. There's utility and nobility in that. However, watch out for work that doesn't serve anyone. (See the movie *Office Space* for great examples of that. It's a great comedy, too.)

Work smart, not hard.
Let's bring that concept back.

Some hard-driving business gurus are quite popular and appear very successful. With sweaty, machine gun patter that promises riches, Lamborghinis and cabin cruisers, they demand that you work both smart *and* hard. Ninety hours a week? That's nothing! What are you? A weakling who needs sleep? Well, yes, in fact, you *are* human. You are not a machine. Forty hours a week is not nothing. It's a big chunk of your life, actually.

Sorry to break it to you. If you do strive to emulate one of these lucky outliers, be careful that you don't break under the strain. Some gurus promote agendas that are...how can I put this nicely? They are unhelpful. They tell you to work harder but that's really all they have to offer.

I know a self-appointed guru who is constantly telling writers to work hard. He doesn't offer a lot of specific advice as to how to achieve goals. He's more of a yell and crack the whip kind of guru. After a while, that grates on my nerves and I shut him off. Most writers I know already work very hard. In fact, most everyone I know works very hard. How many people do you know who can afford to be lazy and still eat? Not many.

To have three jobs in order to barely make a living is *not*, as President George Bush once said, the American Dream. It shouldn't be anyone's dream. That's too much labor with not enough time to enjoy our non-working life.

Don't do the busywork thing.

Turn the page for three handy-dandy guidelines to help you evaluate where to spend your time.

What's Worthy of Your Time and Energy?

I suggest you evaluate your activities based on three criteria:

Learning.
Improving through doing.
Utility to you and others.

Here's how to get there and why:

Someone snarky once said that experience allows us to recognize the mistakes we are repeating. I suggest you learn from others' mistakes. Emulate their successes.

If we only learn from our mistakes, our progress will be slow and painful. Reframe stressful experiences by looking at them as learning opportunities. Imagine how relaxed you could be if you are less attached to outcomes. Think of what comes next as useful experimentation. Experiments don't fail. They get you closer to what works.

Take my example. I drove myself a little mad for 20 years. Every April, I'd worry about reporting and paying my taxes. I hate accounting so I made it a much more stressful experience than it needed to be. I read about tax law. I researched various programs to find the best one to track and record all my receipts.

I can't say I enjoy doing taxes now. It still feels like homework. However, I am much more relaxed about this chore. It's a necessary evil and, when I changed my attitude about the process, I made it less complicated. These days, I dutifully record the columns of numbers. When it becomes more complex than that, I hand off the paperwork to my accountant. She's trained in this nonsense. I leave the heavy calculations, loopholes and confusing forms to the expert.

Any skill is difficult to acquire at first. With repetition, what was once frustrating can even become enjoyable. Just don't try to learn the ropes all at once at the last minute.

Everyone is afraid to look like a beginner when they take up a new skill, sport or unfamiliar endeavor. Tell yourself you are going to figure it out. Everyone who is an expert on anything today once didn't know a damn thing about things that are simple to them now.

When you're doing something new, give yourself permission to suck at it. That's how nervous beginners become relaxed old pros. They don't expect perfection, only improvement. Winners are the ones who keep showing up to practice. Keep showing up to practice.

Finally, a few exploratory questions about the utility of your activities to you and others.

1. Are your habits, hobbies, activities and choice of work serving you and/or others?

2. If your work only serves others, how long can you continue before you hate life, hate others and burn out?

3. If your work only serves you, how are you going to get paid? If you are in a position where you only serve others, what benefits can you gain that will nurture, nourish and sustain you?

4. If your activities do not serve you and they don't serve others, what's your plan to do something else?

For some, they will be easy and breezy. Most will be haunted by these questions until they can come up with better plans as to how they spend their waking hours. Take your time with these questions. Write down your answers.

Do the thing that serves you and is good for someone else, too.

Hack a Better Life

Use cues to trick yourself into getting things done that will improve your energy and decrease your stress.

Here are a few examples of useful cues:

1. Take a deep breath and consciously relax your neck and shoulders every time you touch the handle on the fridge.

2. Shrug your shoulders every time you go through a doorway.

3. Have a shower and brush your teeth rather than eating dessert.

4. Stretch during commercials.

5. Stay in a calf raise for up to two minutes while you brush your teeth.

Anything that you do on a regular basis can be used as a cue. By using this simple life hack, you'll achieve greater consistency and better results at whatever you turn your mind to.

Cues integrate your efforts at self-improvement into your day. Their use illuminates the resistance people often feel when they attempt to institute exercise regimens into their daily routines.

Imagine what exercise and self-improvement tactics you might pair with the following cues: Checking the time, stoplights, washing your hands, looking at the screen on your phone and checking email.

What if you resolved that every time you watched a television program you committed to a yoga pose instead of sitting on the couch? Or performed deep abdominal breathing to relax at stoplights?

Cues are power moves and incredibly effective at getting stuff done that you would not otherwise make time for. Try them. In fact, turn the page to make a plan.

Do the cue thing.

Plans Work Best When They Are Written Down

Stress Buster

Make a list of three cues you could enact immediately and incorporate into your daily routine. Put this short list in a place you will see it to remind you to act on it. For instance, a Post-it note on the bathroom mirror could remind you to do calf raises while you brush your teeth.

Put your cue and the action you'll marry it with here, too, for reference:

Cue:

Action:

Cue:

Action:

Cue:

Action:

Do the things you plan.

Triggers are the Opposite of Cues

For smokers, the cue to light up is often preceded by finishing a big meal. Others are too quick to anger when encountering a slow driver ahead of them.

Cues that do not serve you are triggers and you should make yourself aware of your unconscious behavior. Habits, peer pressure and advertising have hijacked our brains so we often act automatically. Don't act on auto-pilot. Act consciously.

One way to become more aware of unconscious behaviors is to write them down. Keep a food diary and record what you eat in the run of a day. You may find that you eat more and more unhealthily than you thought you did.

Salt, fat and sugar promoted constantly by the food industry also trigger cravings. Even the bright colors of fast food restaurants are designed to get you to eat more (and badly). The drive-through on the way to work is a trigger that hijacks your brain. Do you really want or need that coffee on the way to work, or are you on auto-pilot? Is it possible to go to the movie theater and not eat a huge box of overpriced popcorn?

Somewhere there's a reader who just got a sudden urge to go to a crappy movie just for the buttery popcorn. Replace the urge with something else. Go have a shower. Change into pajamas for the evening. Keep reading this book!

Now that you've brought the unconscious trigger up to the level of awareness, do what you must to break patterns that fail to serve your time and energy.

Some skeptic somewhere is asking, but how do I make myself aware of unconscious triggers? Fair question. Let's explore that next.

Do the Batman thing.
Be a detective.

Detect Your Triggers

When our brains are hijacked, we make unconscious decisions that do not serve us. It's often only after the craving is sated that we become aware of our mistake. How often have you eaten too much and afterward felt regret? "I can't believe I ate the whole thing," or, "I was so hungry but now I feel awful."

To detect our triggers, we have to think about these issues at the right time. Introspection is best done when you aren't under the influence of unconscious forces. That's a fancy way of saying, "Do not shop at the grocery store while you are hungry." Slow down before you take action. Are the peanut butter cups on your grocery list? Then why are they in your shopping cart?

You probably already know many strategies you want to act on. If it's about diet and weight loss, you already know to eat more vegetables. What you may not have is a plan.

To identify your triggers, think about how you want to live, work and feel. Think about what you're doing daily that does not propel you to how you want to be.

Stress-busting action steps:

1. Write down what you need to do.

2. Make a plan.

3. Replace your triggers with helpful cues.*

4. Measure your progress because that which is not measured will not improve.

5. Learn and correct your course as necessary.

6. Repeat.

When you fail (and you will) don't curse yourself and go off the plan. Return to the plan.

*Remember: a trigger is the opposite of a cue. Cues are your keys to replacing the behaviors that do not serve you.

Do the review thing and repeat daily.

But How Do I Feel More Relaxed?

There are many ways to find relaxation and deepen it (all discussed in later chapters, of course.) You could move to dispel excess energy and exercise to increase your energy, for instance. But what about an instant brain hack?

First, let me show you how you can fool your brain right now.

Close your eyes.

Take a deep breath.

Imagine a lemon.

Imagine the weight of the lemon in your hands.

Note the feel of its bright yellow peel across your fingertips.

Tip it to your nose and imagine the fresh, citrus smell.

Now put this imaginary lemon on a cutting board.

Take a sharp knife and slice into it.

See the lemon juice squirting out.

Smell the intensified aroma of citrus.

In your mind, bring the lemon to your lips.

Take a big bite of lemon.

POW! Taste that lemon flavor!

Did you wince? At the very least, your salivary glands started working really hard, didn't they? That's the power of your mind coupled with the power of suggestion. That's why nightmares are so disturbing and why you can get sexually aroused when you are alone. Your brain does not distinguish well between the real and the imaginary.

You really can trick your brain to aim your life in new helpful directions.

Do the following deceptively simple thing.

What does relaxation feel like to you?

When was the last time you felt truly relaxed? At the beach, allowing the sun and sand to warm you? In a pine forest walking on a carpet of green moss and breathing fresh air? Are you happy and relaxed strutting along to upbeat music?

What does this experience of relaxation feel like in your body? Do you notice your shoulders are down and loose instead of up around your ears like earrings? Have you got a confident swagger going on? Are you smiling? Breathing deeper? Are the muscles in your shoulders, hands, feet and calves looser when you are relaxed?

**Remember your experience of relaxation
so you can return to it.**

Your brain differentiates poorly between reality and fantasy. That sounds like a deficit and it definitely can be. However, you can also use that power to your advantage. You are who you pretend to be. I'm going to guess someone reading that suggestion feels resistance but most of us are already pretending. The life we show on Facebook isn't real. It's an idealized version of our lives. There aren't photos of you scrubbing toilets or grocery shopping or doing tiresome chores.

Your brain sends signals to your body and muscle tension builds under stress. Think of your body and mind as an integrated: the bodymind. Not only does your mind affect your body but your body affects your mind. Use that feedback loop. Change the response to stress signals by remembering your feelings of relaxation. Get back in touch with that relaxed state whenever you need. If you find it difficult to focus on relaxing your bodymind in response to stress, you can pump up the signal to relax with gentle stretching, yoga or other exercise.

You can change your mood and experience of the world by changing where you focus your attention. If your stress is mild to moderate, your mindset and stress score will change.*

**Do the thing where you practice remembering
relaxation.**

*If these tactics don't work for you right away, it may require practice. If they don't work at all, no worries. There are plenty more stress-busting strategies ahead to get you in touch with relaxation. If your stress is beyond moderate, please reread the chapter *Caution. Proceed Carefully*.

Stress is Managed, Not Controlled

There are plenty of gurus who will tell you all sorts of silly things. For instance, there once was a business consultant who reasoned that if employees could go without making a mistake for one minute, they could go without errors for three minutes. Then ten, an hour and so on. According to his hypothesis (and against human nature) there was no need for anybody to make a mistake ever again. Yeah, right.

Believe it or not, this business advice was quite popular for a short time. Expensive corporate seminars were held. Many books were sold. Alas. Humans being humans, this strategy was quite disconnected from reality.

Then Scott Adams made fun of the idea in a *Dilbert* cartoon. In the strip, Dilbert points out to the pointy-haired boss that in striving to avoid errors, he's paralyzed by his fear of making any decisions. Nothing much gets done when you work from fear.

Once it was held up for ridicule, corporations moved on to paying another guru thousands of dollars for seminars on new fads.

So it is with stress management. Humans being humans, remember that we do not really control stress. We control variables. We *manage* stress. Stress control was once a more popular idea. It didn't survive meeting real people.

If you live a reasonably long and ordinary existence, things are going to happen that you're not going to enjoy. You'll get called for jury duty when you can't even spare the time to explain why you can't attend jury duty. People will want things at inconvenient times. Medical stuff will probably happen eventually.

You do not control everything and you shouldn't even try. But the illusion of control is a very seductive idea. Remember, though: control is not real.

Very few winners will admit that luck played a part in their amazing success. I'm not trying to denigrate the value of the hard work of the successful. I am pointing out that many factors go into any enterprise's success. Those variables are never under one person's control.

My father came up with an idea that should have made him a millionaire many, many times over. He owned two lumber mills and behind those mills sat mountains of sawdust. What if, he thought, we molded all that sawdust and made fire logs that would catch fire easily in a wood stove? Someone else went on to make millions out of that idea decades later. It was a good idea, but far ahead of its time. He couldn't find investors for the project and he went on to success with other businesses. The variable was that he came in too early and no one was receptive to the idea.

There are many precedents for this. Jello was a product no one could sell until the company gave away thousands of recipe books. People got the idea that they could indeed eat this weird shaking gelatin.

Bizarrely, the screw was invented long before the screwdriver.

What does this have to do with stress management?

The key takeaway is that you must not worry about that which is not under your control. I know, I've said it before. It's so important, it's worth repeating. How many things are you worrying about that are beyond your control? How's that strategy working for you?

Let me translate that into an inspirational poster for your wall: You cannot control the ocean but you can surf the waves.

Okay, back to reality:

There are variables in life. Everyone gets ill from time to time. Everyone faces challenges. This does not mean your success will be denied. It may be delayed, however.

If you're trying to *control* everything, including your stress, you're setting yourself up for failure. High maintenance people who insist on perfection at all times are angry people who become pariahs. Perfectionism is a form of self-hatred. Let it go. Replace that less useful strategy with working on the challenges you can control. Being proactive and positive will keep you plenty busy. No need to wallow in that other stuff.

Life isn't fair but, fear not, our mission is to try to make it fair.

Repeat after me:

I will not freak out, stress out, be angry or otherwise act out about those things I cannot control. That which I can do, I will do. That which I cannot do is not my concern.

Got it? Great. Repeat this as often as you need to in order to make it a life motto.

Do the thing that works over and over.

Put Yourself to the Test

Suppose a coworker is speaking to you in a way that is unfair, rude and condescending. Their manner is coarse and off-putting. Let's deal with the problem effectively.

First, if you are going to cry in the bathroom, save that for later. Do not let them see you sweat. Tell them how you feel. Do not show them. Remain calm or try to appear to be calm so the problem does not escalate. When others speak louder, sometimes the quickest way to put a pin back in that grenade is to speak softer and identify what's happening, if not for them at least for your benefit.

When people are aggressive, it feels like things are speeding up, doesn't it? It feels like you should have a proper response in the moment, thinking on your feet and rising to the occasion.

That's a stress trap.
To fix it, shift your expectation.

Maybe you can formulate the perfect response in the moment. However, when we're under attack, often we don't respond as well in that crucial moment as we wish we had. You might respond in a way that escalates the situation. Later, you might come up with the perfect putdown, a better solution or regret not offering an olive branch.

We have all had the experience of what the French call, "L'esprit d'escalier." The specificity of this phrase is wonderful. Literally, it describes how you feel when the perfect response comes to you as you're leaving the scene of the confrontation. Poised on the stairs, you come up with the script you wish you had so you could replay the scenario to your advantage.

"I wish I'd said x," or, "I should have replied y." Torture, isn't it? There are several ways to handle this situation so you have that answer. Another option is to choose not to respond at all, if you can do that.

Do the self-defense thing.
Turn the page.

Deal with Difficult People

The original title for this chapter was *How to Deal with Difficult People (without murdering them)*. Let's put criminal suggestions to one side, shall we? Instead let's tackle the issue like this:

It's not your job to put every unhinged person back on their hinges.

1. Where possible, handle the exchange in an email. This leaves a paper trail that tends to keep bullies more civil and makes everything clearer. There will be no doubt who said what and it will be on the record in case you need to bring in a mediator. Also, many of us are better at formulating thoughts via the written word (and we stammer much less).

Be warned: Emails don't have a tone of voice like a phone call does. Write with clarity so your good intentions are not misinterpreted.

2. For problems that recur, have a script. That way, you're ready with a prepared response ahead of time. Try to keep it simple and realistic, though. I don't want you lying in bed awake at night playing out endless unlikely arguments in your head. Sleep is too important for that. We all win the imaginary arguments. We lose energy when we become preoccupied with battling ghosts.

3. Similarly, with a conflict in the workplace, be aware of the policies already in place. If there are no such policies, it's time to set the ground rules and you can have a part in that formulation. For instance, you might say, "No, we can't do this or that because it's against our policy." Or, "there's no precedent for that." Or, "that action could set an unfair precedent."

A little planning for objections and problems ahead of time can avoid a lot of trouble. It's important that standards of behavior and protocols for getting things done in the workplace are laid out. This helps everyone manage their behavior and rise to expectations.

4. Have a rationale handy but only if you really need it. Resist the urge to explain too much. State the policy, not how it came to be, starting with the history of the ancestral records of our forefathers.

When you're sure the other person is the one who's being unreasonable, let them explain themselves. When they've had their say, try, "No, I think I'll go in another direction." If someone is wrong about something, that often becomes more apparent the more they speak. In other words, hang them with their own rope.

5. When someone takes an adversarial stance, they're not having a conversation anymore. They're talking at you, not with you. Identify when that happens to control the tenor of the conversation and get back on track. A conversation is not a monologue by the prosecution.

6. If they start talking louder, you might tell them you can hear them fine and there's no need for them to raise their voice. When they repeat themselves, it's time to wind down the interaction. Don't allow them to talk in circles. Focus on a resolution, not who is right and who is wrong. (You're my reader, so I'll assume you're always right about everything.)

7. If they try to bully you or manipulate you emotionally, you might tell them it's time for you to step back. Tell them you'll be willing to speak with them again when they're feeling more objective. "I just walked in and said good morning and I feel like you're coming at me like a cop breaking up a bar fight. Let's give it some more thought before we sit down to talk about this calmly."

8. When we are reactive, we escalate. When we're dealing with a rude person, we can choose to kill them with kindness.

A colleague of mine dealt with difficult people by redoubling her efforts to get them to like her. We could also choose to refuse to engage rude people. Your job description does not read: punching bag.

Personally, I find I am less reactive and stay objective when I treat difficult people as if they are all patients. We tend to be less objective when dealing with family conflicts. However, you'll always be the reasonable one when you use active listening skills and refuse to inflate, engage or catastrophize.

9. A well-placed joke can defuse a tense situation, if you have the knack for that. If the situation isn't really all that serious, try it. If you have enough history with the person who's acting irritably, an easy reply to most problems is, "You say that like it's a bad thing."

For instance, "The washer is overflowing."
Deadpan: "You say that like it's a bad thing."

If nuclear war has just broken out and you answer to the President, this might not be the time for that.

10. More seriously, identify exactly what's happening in the moment. Use "I" messages like, "I feel uncomfortable and awkward when you demand x of me." Or, "You want both projects on your desk by Wednesday morning. To accomplish that, I'll either need more help or we need to prioritize which project is more urgent."

11. When dealing with a subordinate with a complaint, you can steer things in the right direction pretty quickly with, "I hear and understand the problem. Any ideas about how to solve this?"

12. Remember how I said that time feels like it moves faster when you feel you're under attack? Take a step back and slow the action. There is often no reason to respond immediately. You might say, "I'll take your words under consideration and get back to you after I have some time to mull it over." Or, "I'll give you a decision on that in my morning email." Or how about, "I'll talk to you about that when we're both calm"? Or simply, "I'll get back to you on that."

If they come at you again too soon, repeat, "I'll get back to you on that." Then do it in an email. When someone tries to bulldoze over you, slow the action. If you control the pace and the venue of your response, you'll suck the wind from your adversary's sails.

Of course, they may not be an adversary. Maybe they're stressed, too, spreading their stress around and hoping you'll share their load. In my experience, misery doesn't just love company. It insists on it.

Clarity of thought comes from due consideration, not heated words and hasty decisions. When attacked, slow your roll wherever possible.[1]

When people are agitated, do them the favor by opting to manage the situation, remain calm and deescalate.

And finally, if threatened:

#13. Get away from the person and get to safety. If that's not possible, get witnesses. Contact a supervisor, police or Human Resources, whatever's appropriate to your workplace. If someone becomes irrational, have a script and a plan to follow to maintain your safety.

If cornered and threatened, cooperate until you can fight back with everything you've got. I know you've never read that sort of advice in a stress management book. That's one of the reasons I had to write this one. Stress management is not just an issue for people who feel safe and secure otherwise. Stress management is for everyone. (More on that later.)

Here's my emergency plan, in case you're interested.

"You're raising your voice and I'm not cool with that. We're going to end our interaction now. Meet me at the front desk."

In front of witnesses, my script reads: "I sell my time and my expertise. I do not sell my dignity. Goodbye."

If they do not leave, I have alarms in my office, a secret signal to call 911 and I'm prepared to deal with trouble. To date, I have not had to deal with this sort of stress. I'm very fortunate. Most everyone I deal with is lovely and polite and I give no reasonable person cause for offense. However, I'm ready. That's why I don't stress about this issue.[2] Forewarned is forearmed. No one should be threatened in the workplace, or anywhere else. You do not deserve threats.

Do the safe thing.

[1] Everyone's job is important, but jobs don't all have the same pace. Assess the urgency of each situation realistically and hold on to perspective. Many people act like someone is going to die if all demands are not met instantly. If you are in a job where you must

46

respond quickly to a heated conflict (e.g. police, firefighters and air traffic controllers) fall back on your training.

[2] If you do have a workplace incident that is contentious on any level, I suggest you document it immediately and identify witnesses from whom you can collect statements. That can avoid a ton of trouble, too.

Crucial Questions Part I

In the previous chapter, I reviewed ways you could handle a difficult and unreasonable person. But, what if the unhinged person is you? Are you given to road rage? Are you convinced everyone you meet is an idiot? Are you persecuted at every turn? Does it feel like you're at war with the world? You might be the problem.

Consider this: Are you enjoying your anger too much? If you exercise it all the time, you're getting something out of it. Bullies enjoy power over others. Extremists love to have enemies they can feel superior to. People who see enemies everywhere make enemies. If you're always angry, you're even exhausting your friends. There are better ways of dealing with anger that don't leave you lonely. Angry people don't get to have large support networks. We all need connections. Humans are social animals. We *need* friends.

Aggressive people often dress up their actions with labels that comfort them. They might mistake nationalism or racism for patriotism, for instance.

Self-assessment is the first step to self-regulation.

1. Forget how you feel for a moment. What are you *doing*? Without rationalizing how you act and react to others, just look at your actions. Would you like someone to make those moves on you? Would you enjoy being stuck in an elevator with you? Would you hang out with you at all?

2. Is all your anger and reactivity making the world a better place? Is anger making your life better? You've probably been angry a long time. Is your life any better now than it was a few years ago? Is anger working?

3. Does this quiz make you angry? If it doesn't apply to you, it shouldn't irritate you.

Anger is your cue to do the self-assessment thing.

To be effective and change the world, you probably won't find happiness by going through anger. If you are beginning to suspect

48

I'm talking about you (or if you're really angry at me right now) the help you need is beyond the scope of this book. You need to do some work on yourself with a professional counselor face to face. Many people are ready to help you if you want to change. If you're willing, you will markedly reduce the stress in your life.

The next chapter is mostly blank. You will be asked one question. It may be the most important question you will be asked and, if you answer honestly, it will change your life forever.

Ready? Turn the page.

Crucial Questions Part II

Many of us are the authors of our own destruction. We blame our parents for our problems long past childhood. We don't own our mistakes, our flaws or our problems. It feels better to externalize them. In other words, everything that's wrong with our lives is someone else's fault.

The question that could change your life forever is, how much of your stress is your responsibility?

Write down the problems that are under your control.

Beside each item, list what you could do today to change that stressor.

Do the proactive thing.

Crucial Questions Part III

That last chapter might have been tough on you. Take a deep breath and let's adjust your mindset. I do this here because the list you made in the previous chapter might have been upsetting. It doesn't have to be. I asked about your reaction to stressors you can control so your list should be empowering.

Let me give an example of what I mean. I took a tough anatomy and physiology class. As the professor outlined what lay ahead, one of my classmates broke down in the middle of class. The road ahead seemed too intimidating and scary. She was sure she would fail. "There's so much to learn!" she said.

Meanwhile, I was excited by the curriculum. *So much to learn! So much to master!*

The same stimulus that boosted my energy sucked hers away. You see the same thing on roller coasters. Some people will get on once and never go again. Or they won't get on at all. Others enjoy roller coasters again and again. Note that whichever reaction you have, fear or excitement, it's the same stimulus that led to tears or smiles.

What the person who is not energized does not consider is, it's all just a ride. The classmate who panicked passed the course and is now a very successful health professional. If she had thought of the work as a challenge to rise to instead of an obstacle that could crush her dreams, she would have enjoyed that course more.

But how do you change your mindset?

Ask yourself:

If you think of life as a game instead of war, how might that change your life?

Losing a round of golf sounds much better than losing a battle, doesn't it? The loss of a game isn't that big a deal, is it? If you lose a game, you tell yourself you'll practice more and you'll do better next time. When you see life as a game, new opportunities arise. You can look to others to collaborate and recruit to support your endeavors and build a team. Life as a game implies sportsmanship. If you insist on making each day a battle in the war of your life, you may feel righteous energy but are you really making the world a better place? Are you better or are you just getting your exhilaration from righteousness acceleration?

Let's suck the anger and vitriol out of the day, shall we? Are you dressing up your fears in anger? People who operate from fear of loss of status, for instance, often present an angry face to the world. Ironically, constant aggression and anger reduces your status in the world.

As a young man, I thought I had to be tough to get respect. I didn't realize that I could get fear out of others but I was not getting their respect. I hope you don't waste years like I did. That much stress feels like a formula for a short unhappy life. Every endeavor does not have to be reduced to win or die.

Warning

If yours is a win or die attitude, you're not really in the spirit of what we're trying to accomplish here, are you? Think on that. If you're finding a problem for every solution, you're not reducing your stress with positivity and proactivity. You're posing, procrastinating and wasting time. Return this book and go read some fiction. Please continue if you're up for experimenting and doing the things.

Crucial Questions Part IV

Are you having any fun?

As a teenager, I worked in my father's store. My dad rarely looked like he was having any fun at work. The experience convinced me I never wanted to work in retail again.

However, business doesn't have to be that way. Many of the entrepreneurs I know are successful in part because they're interested in others, pursue ongoing learning and, get this, they're actually having fun with the social and problem-solving aspects of business.

There is an unfortunate and popular belief that entrepreneurial folk are all nose-to-the-grindstone types, devoid of humor and counting pennies. The business people I know now are fun to hang out with. They are interesting and interested. They listen and think before they speak. Successful entrepreneurs do not fear change. They invest in themselves and their ideas. They are optimistic and engaged folks who see each move as part of a game. Each move that leads toward a dead end is just another experiment that, even if it fails, gets them closer to their goals. They learn from their mistakes but they do not dwell on them. They do not let their fears color the lens with which they regard the world.

To win the game, self-assess to see if your reactions are proportionate to the scale of the problem. Play the game with less irrational fear. Have more fun with the process. People who make millions aren't out to make millions. They're out to make a better and faster product or service. Their focus carries them through to success because they enjoy what they do. The most successful people I know don't do it just for the money. If it were just about the money, they'd quit sooner. They'd be taken down by heart attacks, overwork, burnout or self-satisfaction after earning the first million dollars.

Again, self-assess, self-regulate and plan.

Do you enjoy what you do? If you could do anything, what would it be? What decisions could you make today that will bring you closer to enjoying what you do tomorrow? What do you want to do next? What fun thing can you do next to make that more fun happen?

To get you closer to living the answer, let's start managing things better. Turn the page to start on getting things together.

Projection

Watch out that you aren't playing the victim and needlessly adding to your stress. At the grocery store, a woman ahead of me in line dropped her groceries. The line was long but, with shopping carts in the way, we couldn't help the woman and the cashier gather up her items. We all waited patiently and I thought that was that.

After I paid for my groceries, I saw the woman again near the door. She complained loudly to a store employee, "Everyone was looking at me! They were standing behind me, so impatient and rude!"

No. She put that narrative in her head. She was embarrassed to drop her groceries and she projected anger on the people behind her in line. Projection is a powerful force. It will blind you if you let it. If you're angry at somebody, make sure you have just cause and know why you are angry. Anger is not a bad emotion when it's appropriate. To find out if your anger is appropriate, ask what fear fuels your rage. Does what you feel really match reality?

Do the realistic thing.

Come Down From the Cross

Everybody needs help. That's why we need to be careful what we teach others. Or, as an old roommate once put it, "If you're going to do the dishes for me every time, I'm going to let you."

When we're too critical or too particular about how things get done, we become the person who has to do it or do it over. This is probably an ego boosting sort of thing that communicates to one and all, "I'm essential! Only I can do this right. I am a martyr and you must all bow to me!"

Martyrdom is overrated.

Perfectionism triggers others to withdraw, leaving you to do all the work. Human energy is not infinite so get things going smoothly by sharing the chores. If your kids are old enough to mow the lawn and make their beds to a reasonable facsimile of a decent job, why are you trying to do everything? Don't criticize the wrinkled blankets and corners that aren't tight enough. Catch them doing something right, encourage them, congratulate and thank them.

Everyone responds well to praise. Make a big deal about the behaviors you want to reinforce instead of throwing fits when results are imperfect. Rewarding good behavior is how you train children to go to the potty instead of pooping in their pants.

During his early toilet training phase, my nephew would pop off the toilet every time (with or without producing results) and announce, "Good boy!" We start with the less-than-optimal and improve with practice so that was a good start.

This strategy works for all sorts of things. Don't make the perfect the enemy of the good.

A half-assed job done by someone else is often better than a chore that exhausts your whole ass. Let others do the less-than-perfect thing.

RescueTime

Lawyers and accountants often record their tasks in fifteen-minute increments. This is important for billing, of course. It is also a useful tool for staying on track and on task. Most people won't do this level of recording unless forced to so I'm not recommending it. Depending on the nature of your work, watching metrics too much can be distracting and therefore detract from productivity.

There's another solution that doesn't require that you interrupt your work: RescueTime. RescueTime runs in the background and tracks where you're spending your time. Once a week, you get a productivity score that lets you know how well you're doing.

Here are a few things to keep in mind with RescueTime:

1. I suggest you install the app and ignore its existence for a week. The idea is to get a baseline score so you know how productive you normally are, before the intervention. Brace for a shock.

2. When the score arrives, look at how much time you're spending on non-productive tasks and recalibrate your efforts the following week.

3. The goal is not to get to 100%. You are not a robot. (I know. I wrote a series of books about robots.) If you are trying for 100% productivity, you're aiming for a score that is too high to sustain. A little relaxing down time spent on Facebook and watching Mojo Top Ten lists is not a bad thing. Don't burn out.

Ten minutes off each hour makes the other fifty minutes more productive. Get up and move around.

I consider myself very productive most of the time. I'm far from perfect but I'm always looking for progress not perfection. Perfectionism is a formula for self-loathing, failure and exhaustion. My personal best on RescueTime is 83%. My worst score was 73%. Your mileage, and your goals, will vary.

Do all things with awareness.

Family Calendars

I run my life using calendars. I have a calendar for each of my clinics that allow clients to book sessions with me in the times I've set for availability. I've yet to figure out how I can combine these calendars into one master. Since I work at different clinics on different days and that schedule never changes, it's manageable.

My favorite calendar is my Google calendar. I use this tool to integrate my work life and my personal life. Add your family to the calendar and everybody can find a way to fit into each other's lives. Knowledge is power. It's also translates to less stress.

My work calendar is much simpler than the family calendar. We desperately need to track where the kids are supposed to be at all times. I have teenagers. Their lives are social whirls filled with jobs, music lessons and school. You know the drill. They're busy and they often need a ride. They both have phones which also help us deal with last minute changes and emergencies.

To coordinate all our lives without stress, I ask everyone in the family, "Please don't ask me to remember your schedule. Write it on the family calendar on the fridge door."

I check in each Sunday night about the coming week. I then enter their schedule on my digital calendar to avoid confusion.

Do the check-in thing consistently and make them responsible for letting you know about interim updates.

It's Not All on You

You are not responsible
for the schedules of others.

Don't allow other people to run your day for you. For instance, at my clinics, to help more people (and not make the day too long) I have to stick to my schedule. If someone thinks their 60-minute appointment was for 4 pm and it was set in my calendar for 3:30 pm, they aren't getting sixty minutes. That wouldn't be fair to me or the client in the next time slot.

I've encouraged you to avoid writing down things that are a waste of time. Calendar entries are not one of those things. The calendar you use to organize your time is an important stress management solution. You'll keep the shackles off if you stick to it.

The office in my old church had a sign on the door I cherish: A failure to plan on your part does not constitute an emergency on our part.

For years, I struggled with how to tell someone they were late or that they had missed an appointment. I didn't want to appear rude (even if they were careless and rude). The reasons I was overly polite are unclear to me now. I never want to offend anyone. I'm Canadian, so maybe there's truth in that stereotype. I don't want to be taken for granted or pushed around, either.

Then, in *Star Trek The Next Generation*, Lt. Worf gave me the words I needed. He shows up at O'Brien's quarters and says something like, "I had you on my schedule for 0800 hours."

That's what I say now. "I had you on my schedule for 4 pm. Do you want to reschedule now or call me back?" If they're offended at that, I don't want that meeting, anyway.

I once visited a doctor's office that had a sign by the front counter: *If you abuse the staff, you will not receive an appointment today, or any other day.*

Et voila!
Do the self-respectful thing.

The Other L Word

I sat with my fiancé in pre-marriage counseling. I don't remember a thing about those classes (except I did resent having to take them to get married). The Rev was a friend of mine so that made the requirement easier to tolerate. Over lunch one day, the Rev asked my wife-to-be and I what the most important key to a long and happy marriage was. I wanted to say sex. Instead I suggested, "Love?"

I was wrong. My wife got the right answer immediately. "Laughter."

Find the funny and you're in for a smoother ride. When I was fifteen, I needed surgery. I was terrified. My palms were sweaty. I lay in bed worrying as if worry might help. As an orderly appeared to take me up to the O.R., I discovered something about myself I'd never known until then: under threat of death, I'm hilarious.

I can't remember a thing that I said but, suddenly, I was a joke machine. I got the orderly laughing. The laughter spread to the nursing staff. I soon felt pretty chipper, too. Making people laugh is a power move.

As I left the orderly behind and they got me on the table to cut me open, one of the nurses asked, "How do you know Jay?"

"Who?"

"Jay. The man who brought you up to surgery."

"Oh. I don't know him. We just met."

"I've never heard him laugh so hard."

"Yeah, well, it turns out this life or death situation is part of my origin story. I just found out I have a superpower. I'm worried I discovered it a bit late, though."

"What?" By her eyes, I knew that behind her mask, she was confused. To her, I was spouting gibberish.

"Never mind," I said. "But if I live through this, I want a cape when I wake up. Blue, please. That red Superman cape is a little garish for me. And no red boots. I'll look like a kid in rain boots if they're red."

"Um…"

"Maybe you better get the anesthesiologist in here or I *will* keep talking. Stop me before I kill again!"

I lived. I learned that when I let go of other people's expectations, I can find the funny in just about anything. The Rev was right. A little comedy at the right time makes for a much smoother ride in marriage and everything else.

Do the funny thing.

Truth and Consequences

You're lying to yourself about something. What is it?

That was an ambush, wasn't it? You didn't see that question coming. Sorry, mate, but it's an important question we need to talk about and consider seriously. A lot of stress books focus on behavioral changes. I want to get at the subtext of your life. What is your underlying philosophy? Everyone has one, even if they don't know it. How you think guides your actions so we need to explore that.

So? What are you lying to yourself about? The first thing that comes to mind is the thing you need to deal with first. What came up?

If nothing sprang to mind, here are a few statements that might prime the mind pump. As you take another run at the question, problematic lies may surface. Does anything here strike a nerve?

1. I really am that unhealthy.

2. I'm not as supportive of my children's choices as I should be.

3. I like to think I'm a rebel but maybe that's not true. Is being a rebel working for me?

4. I keep doing the same things and expecting a different result.

5. I tell myself I like who I am but I'm terrified that everyone thinks I'm an impostor.

6. I'm not as good a spouse as I like to think I am.

7. I tell myself that my estrangement from my family doesn't matter but when they reach out to me and I shut them down, I have doubts.

8. I don't have a drinking problem...but why did that question come to mind first when I was asked this question about the lies I tell myself?

9. Am I as thin as I like to think I am?

10. I do not resent my sister. Well...maybe a little.

11. I spend a lot of money I don't have, but I'm under so much stress, I deserve a few nice things. Don't I?

These are just examples of the sort of answer that may come up. Give this question some time and deep consideration. This is the sort of thing I wish we'd covered in philosophy class: real, applicable and uncomfortable. Since university failed me in this regard, this seems like the place to bring it up. Introspection about your lies will often give you the answer you seek. If you can figure out where you're messing up and what you're going to do about that personal inventory, excellent.

**Do the page flip thing to figure out
how you're going to handle this revolution
about the lies you tell yourself.**

Truth & Action

In the previous chapter you asked yourself what comfortable lies you were telling yourself. That got uncomfortable quickly, didn't it? Now make sure you link up the self-evaluation you did with action to resolve that cognitive dissonance. Saying one thing and doing another is a formula for stress. Believing one thing and acting in a contradictory way builds stress. When you are aligned in thought, word and deed, internal struggles are resolved and stress eases.

There are alternatives if, like many of us, you find you do not take action on your revelations:

1. Partnering with a buddy so you have to deliver regular accountability reports is one way to go.

2. Going deeper, working with a therapist might be your ideal way to discover what you are hiding from yourself.

3. A mentor can give you objective feedback.

4. A health support group, online or in person, might be your avenue depending on your individual challenges.

**Do the honest thing and seek help
so you lose the lies that hamper you.**

How to Defuse the Stress Bomb

It would be great to live in a world without consequences.
This is not that world.

When you opt for the rich sugary dessert every day there will be consequences. You probably will not enjoy those consequences. When you put off what you can do today for tomorrow, work is going to pile up and, as the Knights of the Roundtable used to say, "That shall sucketh."

A couple of chapters back, I asked, "You're lying to yourself about something. What is it?" I know many readers didn't try that mental exercise. Some won't at all. Let's try to reach those who will with one quick exercise.

Some of the greatest stressors are the problems that build up in the background, the ones you are trying to ignore and hope will go away. Is it the debt you're hiding from your spouse? Is it the paperwork you're ignoring? Is it the healthier food choices you know you should be making but put off?

Get out a sheet of paper.
Across the top, write
I am lying to myself about:

Next, set a timer for two minutes. For the next two minutes, you will not raise the tip of the pen from the paper. You will write as fast as you can. You must keep the pen moving. Get out of the way of all that second-guessing, self-editing and waffling. Write. Write as fast as you can. That will get your resistance out of the way so you can get to the answers you've been hiding from yourself.

You know you're going to have to deal with the lies you tell yourself eventually. The stress will be less as soon as you get to fixing those issues. Let's identify the problems so you can tackle that stress and make it manageable.

You want to skip past this because it's uncomfortable. That feeling of discomfort is like a red blinking light on a bomb. The faster you hurry on without dealing with this, the bigger the explosion in the end.

Do the fast writing thing.

The Write Solution

Have you completed the previous exercise? Have you identified what you've been lying to yourself about?

Now repeat the frantic pen to paper exercise on another sheet. This new sheet contains all the *actions* you will take to address the issues on the first page. Set five minutes on the timer and...go!

You're already familiar with the challenge of getting an uncomfortable task done. Every April, when taxes are due, the procrastinators descend on hapless accountants with shoeboxes full of crumpled receipts. For a much larger fee than they would normally charge, armies of accountants figure out what could have been easily solved by their panicked clients. That's why the slow and steady approach to keep on top of things is less costly and less stressful. Overcome the short-term pain for the long-term gain. Use your calendar to schedule the maintenance tasks that will ease your overall stress.

Come back to this writing exercise whenever you need it.

1. You're lying to yourself about something. What is it?

2. Now, what are you going to do about that?

3. Identify one small step you could take immediately in the right direction.

4. You know what to do next. Get out your calendar and work backwards from the goal to today's solution, piling up all those small steps back to where you stand today.

5. Repeat as necessary.

Never wait for the thing to explode before you do it. Do the writing thing and take action.

How I Take Action on My Lies

The lies we tell ourselves can be crippling to our efforts at a better life. My support network of choice is a mastermind group. Why mastermind? Because many heads are better than one. The foundation of the relationships you'll build is honest feedback. Without honest feedback, it's a waste of time. A mastermind group will help get you aligned with your goals. Partner with people who are a little farther down the life and career path you desire. That saves a lot of time and reduces a ton of stress.

When I talk to high-powered, motivated and ambitious people, I am motivated. I notice something about these allies. They think very clearly and they tend to speak plainly, sometimes uncomfortably so. However, there is no malice. They're trying to get things right. They're trying to help me solve problems just as I'm trying to help them.

Part of me dreads the feedback some members give. However, the people who have helped me the most are also the most critical. I trust them and they are my friends. To get the most from the mastermind, I have to drop my defenses and truly be open to their aid.

This is not to say that they are always right. I trust my mastermind friends to be honest in their reactions to my ideas. I always take their suggestions seriously. I often act on their advice but I don't substitute their judgment for my own. It's up to each of us to listen to advice, take what we can use and discard the rest. (Just like this book!)

Through the relationships I've built with these heavy hitters, I have improved. I can't know or do everything. My mastermind group has helped me get farther down the road to success than I would otherwise be. The discomfort at where I get things wrong is momentary and the benefits last. It's better to make mistakes within the safety of the group so my embarrassments are not on display when I unveil my work to the world.

What allies might you gather or join to get on track with your journey, whatever that happens to be? It's probably best to join one before you try forming one so you get a good sense of how it works.

You'll give and get. Be prepared to help others. There will definitely be a profitable information exchange but only if the group is honest, kind and open. Trade secrets shared within the group must not be leaked beyond the group. With trust, you'll create an atmosphere that fosters crucial information sharing.

Do the collaborative thing.

When Honesty isn't about Honesty

In the previous chapter, I preached the great worth of a mastermind group. You must have a lot of trust and truth within that group to make it work. Here's how to know if someone doesn't belong in your group or in your life.

RED FLAG

When someone often uses the phrase, "I'm just being honest," they're dangerous to everyone around them. Even if they are right, they're still acting like asses because the root of their criticism isn't an effort to help. What they are is mean. When someone has a habit of being hypercritical without giving any encouragement, their object is not to supply honest feedback. They run others down relentlessly. In order for them to feel good they *must* make you feel bad.

You can see this behavior in reviews and comment threads all over the internet. Monsters and trolls crush everything and they don't care about their targets. When you hear the phrase, "I'm just being honest," from someone in your life, that's likely someone who mistakes brutality for honesty.

Such people aren't helpful. Pay no attention to them. They are haters and that's all they've got. If you become one of their targets, take solace in knowing that every successful person on the planet has a following of haters. Rather than move on to find something they do like, the haters stalk the successful, trying to bring them down a peg.

Director Kevin Smith used to do battle with haters before KA-BLOCKING them on Twitter. All the while, his wife was in the background (lounging in their beautiful home in the Hollywood Hills) asking, "Kevin, why do you care?" Recently, someone went beyond being a critic and said hateful things about his daughter. Smith's response was mature and surprisingly calm. The upshot of his message to the hater was, "You must be very unhappy in your life to do such a low thing." Amazing, right? He stepped back and didn't get sucked in. It's a solid model for how to handle over the top criticism.

I'm the author of more than twenty books so, naturally, there will be those who don't get me. Most readers do enjoy my fiction, for instance, but it's impossible to please everyone. If it makes you feel better about the criticism you receive, have a look at the reviews of the best books you've read and the movies you love. Look at the one-star reviews. Read the reviews from people who think Shakespeare is stupid. Feel better yet?

I read all my reviews but I read the bad ones only once. If you aren't picking up what I'm putting down, you aren't part of my tribe. Sorry if I'm not your thing but I wish you the best in finding something you do like. Humans are tribal. They pick sides. *Star Trek* versus *Star Wars*, Apple versus Microsoft, your baseball team versus their baseball team. It's in the blood. Don't take it too seriously. Honest friends are valuable. Someone who doesn't care about you when they're talking trash is just talking for their own benefit.

I've mentioned Penn Jillette in this book already. (I admit, I'm a fan of his magic.) He once noted that you can have a million fans who love you but it's the one unkind comment you remember. Eventually, Jillette came to realize that fixating on the opinion of one person who doesn't appreciate his work was an insult to the majority who love Penn & Teller.

That sounds wise to me.

Do the things you love for the people who get you.

72

What if You're a Hater?

Are you using "honesty" as a weapon?

1. If you use the phrase, "I'm just being honest," often, ask yourself, "What's my motivation behind criticism?" Is your target trying something you wish you were doing?

2. You get to express your opinion. Sure. And you get a hit of dopamine that makes you feel good, right? Do you care if your target feels bad for a long time? Are you trying to help when you criticize, or are you showing off to prove how superior you are? Does that sound like behavior you would admire if it was directed at you?

3. Do you consider everyone inferior to you? Are you trying to make a better world or are you trying to control it?

4. Has your plain-speaking lost you friends and allies?

5. Are you cut out of discussions at work or at school?

6. Are you the one person in the meeting who can be relied upon to say, "That idea sucks and won't work?" Do you want to be that person, or do you want to be the person who finds a way to perfect ideas and make things work smoothly?

7. Are people happy to see you coming? Or are they stiff and guarded in your company, unwilling to say much? You know fear isn't the same thing as respect, right?

8. Are you happy? What makes you happy? Have you thought about other topics of conversation that don't include gossip and constant criticism? If you didn't talk that way, would you have anything else to say?

9. When you last provided negative feedback, did you find anything to like as well, if only to spare their feelings? Did you really find zero of value in that idea, proposal or book or were you just getting off on acting self-righteous?

10. When you last provided negative feedback, did you tell the person privately, or did you revel in tearing them down publicly?

If you're squirming or even a little angry as you read this chapter, gee, why are you squirmy and irritated? If this is you, stop and reevaluate. If you don't want to stop this behavior for the sake of others, do it for yourself. Here's the thing: people know what you're doing and they don't like you more for it.

Sometimes a hard case will say, "It doesn't matter that I'm disliked. What matters is I'm right!" Sure. You are not a social animal. You aren't human at all. Please, share more information with us from the planet Xorlak. What's that alien planet like where no one cares what anyone else thinks? Sounds like a pretty crappy place to live.

Back to reality: Chuck Wendig wrote a *Star Wars* book. There was quite a storm in social media about it for a number of reasons. It didn't please some fans of *Star Wars* because they didn't feel it was in keeping with the rest of the series. Some didn't like his writing style. Worse, a campaign developed against the book. Numerous reviews objected to gay characters in the story. As the campaign gained steam, the book rocketed up the charts. The more the book was hated, the more reviews it gained. Professional reviewers tended to like the book. That lent credence to the idea that many reviewers' opinions were influenced by homophobia.

More reviews helped the book's sales, whether they were negative or positive. That's a function of the algorithms that drive the marketplace.

More important, reviewers who didn't even read the book or whose opinions were expressed in an over-the-top way (i.e. outrage) are easily dismissed. Similarly, if you're the one at the conference table or in the knitting circle who always has something negative to say and nothing positive to contribute, your peers will dismiss you out of hand, too.

"Christina doesn't like the idea."

"So what? Christina doesn't like anything."

Remember the story of the boy who cried wolf? This is the corollary to that story. The boy lied about seeing the wolf so often that he was ignored when there was real danger. Are you "just being honest," so often it's dangerous? Is this working for you? If this stress applies to you, you're lowering your value.

Fortunately, awareness about how you come across is half the battle. Psychologists call it self-monitoring. Self-monitor and self-regulate your way to a happier you. When you feel the urge to speak the truth, make sure the truth is your real motivation. If you're not sure, repeat the above exercise and go through the questions again, 1 - 10.

You can change. People do it all the time. Just let go of the need to be right. You can still want to get things right without being a jerk about it. The choice is not, "Do you want to be right or do you want to be happy?" You *can* get things right. Simply focus on getting "things" right, not that *you're* right. We can all work much better with others when we delete ego from the equation.

How do I know you can change? Because I've seen it. Because I've seen it in the mirror. You'll change because you want to do so. You're reading this book so we know you want less stress in your life. You have only been hypercritical in the past because you wanted to feel good about yourself. You wanted others to recognize how smart you are. When you add diplomacy to your arsenal and let go of the ego and snark, you will get the love and recognition you deserve.

Do the thing without being a jerk about it.

More Questions About You

Next time you are under stress, observe your reactions. This is about how you see yourself and how you interact with the world. Answer me these questions three:

Are you seeking approval too much?

In my 20s, I felt like I was always waiting for legitimacy from above. I once had a job interview in a niche of the book industry. My potential boss started the interview by saying he wouldn't take me seriously or allow me to have an opinion for seven years. Only after that much time would I be worthy of an opinion.

"Thanks for your time, but I think I'll just go become a neurosurgeon or an engineer at NASA."

It's a freeing feeling when you let go of the idea that you're an adult or an expert only after somebody else sees your value.

Are you grateful for what you have?

When we focus on what we don't have, we're unhappy. When we appreciate our gifts, stress lessens. (Just because it's a trite cliche doesn't make it less true.)

Do you apologize too much?

As a Canadian, it's a cliche that we apologize too much (and often true.) Sorry about that.

An earnest unforced apology to anyone you have transgressed is a fine thing. When it's a way of life, when you say, "I'm sorry," reflexively over nothing, you communicate that you value yourself less than others. Give yourself the gift of more self-respect. Do not pay what you don't owe.

Do the questioning thing.

Combat Sensory Overload

We swim in a sea of information, swallowing it, choking on it, drowning in it. At every turn, people expect instant gratification. They want emails answered immediately. If we do not answer a text within seconds, they wonder what is wrong.

Here's a radical idea: the speed of your modem is not the speed of life. Technology exists to serve us, not the other way around. To combat sensory overload, step back and take a break. Unplug something.

Comedian Joe Rogan made the observation that we get a lot of news that is not relevant to us. News feeds flood in from all over the planet to report on issues that increase your stress but are really beyond your control. (Remember? Don't worry about what you can't control.)

Of course, we should all be informed. However, as life hacker Tim Ferriss points out, if something really important is going down that affects his life, someone in his circle will let him know. If you're going to consume media from all over the world that has the potential to increase your stress, I suggest that you watch and listen actively. Active listeners evaluate incoming messages, always conscious of what can be safely ignored. Listen for signals that change you or that you have the power to affect. The rest is noise.

One easy way to cut down incoming messages that do not serve you is a media fast. Take a Saturday or Sunday and do not go on social media. Delete Facebook and Twitter from your phone. The world will spin on without you watching it for one day. You may feel withdrawal symptoms at first. Try something else non-electronic to fill that time and you will soon forget about social media. Unplug your modem. Go where there is no wifi. (I get a lot of writing done at Starbucks because I don't trust the security of the wifi.)

If you feel naked without your phone, you're wearing it too much. If you are over the age of twenty, you went for years without constant updates beamed at you. Get back to that more often.

Today's exercise:

**As soon as you put this book down,
go do something social in the real world.
Balance out that overwhelming electro-influx.**

Do the quiet thing.

Paralysis by Analysis

Once in a while I run into someone who is not moving forward and taking on new challenges because they think they need more information. They're waiting for everything to be put in place and perfect before they even begin to act.

They say things like, "I just need to read a few more books and do a bit more research." Or, "I can't start a diet now. It's not Monday. I have to wait until Monday." And, "I'll begin to do the things I want to do after I clear off everything on my to-do list."

Procrastination is a recipe for stress. It's tricky, though, isn't it? Doing a little more research certainly sounds like a cautious and productive thing to do. Check your motivation. Do you really need more research or are you holding yourself back from getting things done due to fear of failure?

Life can be very short. Do not wait for perfect. You will be waiting for a long time and hating yourself while you wait. Perfectionism's real name is self-hatred.

What to do instead of procrastinating:

1. Jump in and figure out the minimum you need to know to get started.

2. Find a mentor to speed up and flatten out the learning curve.

3. Learn what you need to learn to begin your new diet or your new business or your new exercise program or whatever, but get started. Put it on your calendar and make time for the learning and doing process.

4. Begin as soon as possible. It doesn't have to be perfect. It needs to start.

This reminds me of a saying about books and art: Art is never finished. It is only abandoned. Do not be so precious about your work. Get it done and get it out there. Stick to your schedule and do not be so easy on yourself. It's called a deadline, not a liveline. Stop moving the deadline back and get it done on the schedule you set.

Excuses don't make you happier.
Excuses don't make money.
Excuses don't work.

Do the thing.

Understanding Anxiety

A friend of mine was in crisis. His social anxiety had built a wall so high that he couldn't see a way out. My friend slid down an emotional spiral in which he could not work.

When people feel overwhelmed in this way, it's often difficult for others to understand. When you're on the couch paralyzed by a tension headache, for instance, your responsibilities don't necessarily stop when you do. You try to power through. However, not all illnesses can be powered through. Anxiety isn't like a tension headache and it certainly isn't laziness. In fact, anxiety takes up an astonishing amount of energy.

I have to tell you, people are often more willing to help out than you might think. In the midst of depression and anxiety, you may feel alone but you really aren't. Give people a chance to help you and many will. It's so common a problem that societal awareness and sensitivity is on the upswing.

In my friend's case, deadlines slid by and that only made him feel worse. He could not work. He worried people would not understand. Then he got the nicest message from one of his clients. Basically, the message was:

1. I hope you feel better soon.

2. Don't add misplaced guilt to your anxiety. Let's keep this disappointment in perspective. I'll be fine. You are late with work but you are not late with my organ transplant.

3. I know you're a really nice person and if you could work through this problem right now, you would. I understand that you can't.

4. When you're feeling better, I look forward to working with you again.

In a few words, my friend received the message that he still had value, was liked and cared for whether he could work or not.

If you watch the news too much, it's easy to get angry and sad. It's easy to forget that people can destroy your cynicism with one kind act. Beautiful, isn't it?

Do the calm thing.

Random Hint for Parents with Headaches

If you have young children, they often don't understand headaches. When Mommy or Daddy doesn't feel up to playing, they're still raring to go. Try putting a bandaid on your forehead. Little kids understand ouchies when a bandage is involved.

They may cut you some slack as you lie on the couch. They might even give your forehead a kiss and give you a loving snuggle. This won't always work but when it does, it's the sweetest thing in the world.

Do the sweet things.

Another Weird Question

What are you getting out of being stressed all the time?

We are very clear that we don't want bad stress in our lives. Oddly, we often open the door to it when it knocks. We still go to the non-obligatory meetings of the Chronically Distressed Club. We still have lunch with club members who love to clang alarm bells. We still do things that we'll complain about later. We hang out with people who pressure us into doing things we don't want to do. Why?

Are these really obligations you can't dodge? Or maybe, just maybe, are you getting something out of it? There are many ways we volunteer to count ourselves among the Chronically Distressed. Perhaps it's a confusion between doing a lot of things versus actually getting things done. Maybe it's the drama and urgency over the paperwork (done or left undone). What's the negative experience that you could replace with a positive one? Could you squeeze out that little adrenaline shot using exercise, chasing children through corn mazes at Halloween, or doing the thing that truly excites you?

Remember that eustress is the sort of stress that gets you up and going in the morning. Eustress is fine. Eustress connotes ambition to achieve and dials in to that sense of urgency we all need when we're doing anything of utility. Eustress shows you care enough to serve others swiftly and well.

The mire of distress is what we are usually talking about. That's the kind of stress we need to manage. Distress and eustress can feel similar, but eustress actually serves you. Distress hurts you. How about it? What have you experienced today? Eustress or distress? Are you taking care of business, or are you getting pushed around by busyness?

**Please do the answer my question thing
(not for my sake but for yours).**

A Short Chapter I Wish Was Unnecessary

Do not put up with abuse.

It is never worth it to stay in abusive relationships. Find a way out of abusive situations and stay out of danger.

There is nothing you can change about yourself to appease an abusive person. Don't argue. Don't try to change them. As soon as it is possible, escape to safety. Don't go back.

**You are not a thing
to which things should be done.**

Thought and Action

My wife is a respected psychologist. I call her She Who Must Be Obeyed so you can tell I take her seriously. I asked her to dumb down Cognitive Behavioral Therapy (CBT) for me. "Basically, it's thought followed by action. Cognitive equals thought. Behavior equals action. So, do what you say you'll do."

"Huh? Make it dumber for me," I said. "There must be more to it than that."

Heavy sigh. "If you're freaking out that you can't do something, you change what you're telling yourself to reflect your goals. You tell yourself that you can do x or y and then you follow through and do it."

"Oh. And does it follow that if I change my behavior, that will also change my thoughts?"

My daughter was listening. "Sure," she said. "Like if you're feeling unhappy and you smile anyway, you fool your brain into thinking you're happier."

That's the simple version in a few paragraphs. Interestingly, CBT has been helpful in cases of social anxiety. If you suspect you need a psychologist or psychiatrist, pick up the phone and get help.

Do the therapeutic thing.

Journaling

You may find it therapeutic to write down what's going on in your life. We often express ourselves better when we write. (If you ever meet me in person, I tend to stammer and say, "um.") Writing clarifies our thoughts, not just to others but for ourselves, too.

We used to call this exercise keeping a diary. However, since that evokes images of young girls in pigtails, adults call it journaling. Some people even blog their lives. As a writer, any time I spend writing tends to go toward the next book. However, I know several people who benefit from writing "morning pages," a simple idea that became a movement popularized by Julia Cameron, author of *The Artist's Way,* in 1992.

Some write in the morning and chronicle how they feel, what they plan for the day or anything else that occurs to them to write. The thrust of Cameron's book was to reconnect with our creative energies. I find writing meditative so I certainly see the benefit of journaling.

A friend told me that she kept a journal for years and, by rereading it, she discovered she was dealing with many of the same relationship habits and emotional issues at thirty-something that she had complained about in college. It was instructive in showing her how she might try new things to move forward and break her old patterns.

Someone else I know tracks goals on a monthly basis. Some entrepreneurs are fans of long-term goals, writing down five-year plans and whatnot. A lot can happen in five years. For most people, planning like that is impractical and four years too long. I wouldn't worry about planning in detail any further than a year ahead. Just work on the variables you can control instead of attempting to see too far into the future with a crystal ball.

If you use your journal as a planner, refer to it often so you are more likely to act on your ideas. If it's a journal of your life, instead of just recording events, include how you feel. Look for trends. Are things generally getting better or worse? Use the clarity found in writing to unearth what's holding you back from the better life you want to create.

Do the clear-headed thing.

Checking In

We're pretty far into the book, aren't we? Have you been doing the exercises? Tried anything new?

Take this opportunity to rate your pain, stress and energy on a scale of 1 - 10.

Have you noticed a change from the beginning of the book?

Imagine those pain, stress and energy scales as a line, like this:

PAIN

----

1   5   10

STRESS

----

1   5   10

ENERGY

----

1   5   10

Where does your pain, stress and energy fall on each of these lines? Mark the first spot on the line that feels right. (1 is the least pain and stress you've ever felt. 10 is the worst. 1 is the least energy you've ever felt. 10 is the most.)

Now, ask yourself, if you made that mark an arrow, which way would it be pointing? Are things getting better or worse? Are you more optimistic or less? If things are getting better, congratulations! I'm glad things aren't as bad as you might have thought.

This is an awareness exercise. Whether things are getting better or worse, you may still need to get professional help. Do you need help? You know it's okay if you need help, right? Needing help doesn't mean you are weak. Needing help means you are tired and you are human. Asking for help is a strong move. It's the way to turn your arrow in a better direction.

Do the best thing for you.

Adjust Expectations to Reality

Why, I wonder, do so many people expect everything to come easily? I am a big fan of caper movies. *Sneakers, The Italian Job, Oceans 11*? I *love* those kinds of movies. If it's got a heist, I'm there. However, whenever I see a cat burglar whose drill is always fully charged and the screwdriver fits the screws, I know it's a fantasy.

I bought a barbecue one afternoon intending to use it that night. I had help from a friend named Van. Between the two of us, Van and I are well educated and reasonably capable. We were so optimistic when we started this little domestic project. What fools we were.

I pulled the barbecue, in all its many pieces, out of the box. I placed the components on the patio and reviewed the instructions to confirm that I had everything I would need. I was sure I'd be cooking in short order. Then Van and I began to sweat. There was cursing and laughter. Holes for screws did not line up the way I imagined they should.

It was 8 pm and beginning to get dark when my wife called out from the kitchen window. She wisely gave up on the two of us and ordered Chinese food. If Tom Cruise was constructing a barbecue in a *Mission Impossible* movie, he'd have it together in a jiffy (all to a rockin' soundtrack). He would light the propane as the pounding music score reached its crescendo. That's not real life.

Still, a lot of us walk around expecting that things are easier than they are. We expect every deadline to be met smoothly, never encountering an obstacle, illness or delay. We think others should complete their jobs faster even if we have no idea what those jobs may entail. We are impatient with others and with ourselves when these expectations prove unrealistic.

Entitlement is another way we confuse an Ought with an Is. If everything was as easy as we hope, success and riches would be for everyone, everywhere, all the time. Do not burden yourself with entitlement and don't breed it in your children. Optimistic realism will carry you further and allow you to sustain your energy.

Build an expectation of unforeseen delays into your plans. You won't wake up and be out of the house in only five minutes. It will take longer to complete this or that project. Realistic deadlines reduce stress.

On the other hand, don't let this knowledge dumb down your expectations *too* much. The expression, "life's not fair," is often used as an excuse for inaction. I prefer the corollary to this expression: Life may not be fair but it's our responsibility to make it that way.

**Unreasonable people are the ones
who change the world.
Do that crazy ambitious thing
in a reasonable way.**

Living Small

When we are young it seems like we have all the time in the world. There is much to do but there's also less pressure to begin. We have time to prepare, to dream and to fantasize. We don't understand the hurry that older people are in. We even stretch out childhood to make it last longer so we don't have to face adult responsibilities. If we prolong our developmental stages too long, we set ourselves up for failure.

And so we come to living small. You have big dreams. Is real life matching those dreams? Often, our reality and our fantasies about how life should be diverge drastically. If you're in that gap, read on.

Failure and disappointment pave the road to success. I have written books that I thought should have been bestsellers. They weren't. I have operated businesses that I thought should have been bigger and more successful. I thought I'd be more successful than I am by now.

Read that last sentence again:
I thought I'd be more successful than I am by now.

The first problem here is entitlement. I've covered that in the previous chapter, so I won't repeat it here. Just keep in mind that, though life is not fair we are supposed to try to make it that way. It's not going to be easy. If it were easy, everyone would have the success they feel they deserve.

But I have good news. Let me tell you about a friend of mine to illustrate my point. He's a comedian. He has already written for television and performed internationally. He's a brilliant man, quick and funny and big-hearted. He's also been beaten down by life a bit. He's had a lot of heartaches and setbacks. It's a good thing he's hilarious about it. He's been in a holding pattern. He's taken jobs that he could do but those jobs didn't have anything to do with performing comedy in front of appreciative crowds. Those jobs did not harness his talents. They did not feed his dreams.

Here's the good news for him and for the rest of us. He spoke to his fans and asked for help. He encouraged his support network to hold him accountable in changing his life. It's working. He's lost a lot of weight by dieting and working out. It happened in large part because he made such a public commitment to weight loss.

He didn't have a lot of dough but he knew he needed to work with a psychotherapist. He asked for help and is getting it. He knows he has to get head shots, go to auditions and pursue voiceover work. He knows he has to get out and do standup in front of crowds again. He has to work at it daily and weekly to align his gargantuan talent and ambition with his work. He knows all this now. I have no doubt he will succeed.

Chances are excellent that you already know what you have to do to change your circumstances. You're reading this book so you've probably got problems. You already have the solutions you need, too. All you have to do is act.

If you already have your solutions but you haven't acted on them yet, pull up your calendar and work backward from your goal. What can you do today to advance your plans?

Write what you're going to do to align your thoughts, your words and your deeds. Return to this exercise daily. It's past time to align word, thought and deed. You know this. You've got this.

Do the thing you know you have to do.

A Terrifying Question

How many of your ideas are really your own?

The simple answer is probably: frighteningly few. We are conditioned to believe many things from an early age. Much of our brainwashing is so ingrained we don't even think of it as brainwashing. For instance, suppose you're born in a Christian community and your family is Christian. You grow up with church as a fact of life that is taken for granted. The church is the center of your community. It is natural that you would believe everyone should believe as you do. Your tribe cares about you and no one is trying to deceive you.

This experience is so common, the perspective of other cultures is rarely, if ever, considered. Following up on the example above, if you had been born in another culture, chances are excellent you would not be Christian, or at least wouldn't take it for granted. We accept the lives we are born into and we don't question the rules and customs we are surrounded with.

I'm not picking on Christianity. The same is true of many beliefs. How we live betrays the subtext of our beliefs. We are influenced by our families, our peers and our communities. Look to your friends and they'll generally reflect what you believe is true, false and possible.

My point is not to refute any particular belief system. My purpose here is to ask if yours is an examined life. I majored in journalism and minored in philosophy. I've become severely disenchanted with the state of journalism. Similarly, my philosophy classes (at least any of a more contemporary nature) were a huge disappointment. Most contemporary philosophers in academia don't seem interested in exploring how to live. They are averse to such simple declarative statements as, "I think, therefore I am." They ask, "Yeah, but how do you know you think?" Then they get sucked down semantic rabbit holes that test the student's patience but provide no illumination. A career in philosophy was once an inquiry into capital-T Truth. Now, it's book reports on what other philosophers think.

To the key question, I ask again, how many of your ideas about how to live were arrived at through evaluation? How much of how you live now was simply inherited and conveyed through social osmosis?

This is not to cast aspersions on your parents, your culture or your beliefs. I'm asking honestly, which expectations that rule your life are your own? What if you examined those assumptions and figured out that you don't want to do what you were told?

This is so important, it's time for a quick foray into confronting the big choice: To be or not to be. This isn't about Shakespeare. It's about all of us.

Do the thinking thing.

Dig Up the Roots of Your Truth Part I

Let's imagine you are starting your life over again. You could, you know. It's not too late. Let's examine the basis of your assumptions. Try these questions:

1. Do you believe there is only one star-crossed lover whom you will find and love to the end of time?

2. Are you suited to marriage, or will you always wonder if there is someone better suited to you elsewhere?

3. Do you assume that, in order to live the life you want to live, you must get an undergraduate degree? A PhD? Some other specific training?

4. What does a happy life look like for you? Is it a house, a spouse and five children? Is it a life without children?

5. Is your life on hold because you can't leave a specific place or person?

6. Will you be successful only if you are rich? Do you think poor people are inferior?

7. Where do you want to live? Where must you live? If you love the place where you vacation, have you considered living there? If not, why not?

8. Do you believe your career arc should be working hard until you have earned the right to coast a little and then, after two or three weeks vacation each year, eventually retire on the nest egg you've built? Could you follow Tim Ferriss into the *4 Hour Work Week* and live rich now in the Philippines?

9. Is travel something only other people can afford? Is it possible you could work less and enjoy life more in the present? Is happiness something that must always be put off?

10. Do you have to work for someone else? When are you old enough to change that? At what age is it too late to change? How many years

do you have to age or "pay your dues" before you get to have a valuable opinion? At what age do you consider yourself an autonomous person?

11. What does success mean? Having one career path that's always pointed up? Fame? Riches? The biggest house on the block?

12. If you were offered a sailing trip around the world, would you be excited or is your first response to come up with reasons why you can't do it?

13. Is there a God? If so, what are you certain is true about the deity?

14. Is forgiveness for everyone? Is love for everyone?

15. What do you believe about yourself? What do others believe about you that you only wish were true?

16. Should money be hoarded until you're fabulously wealthy? How wealthy do you have to be before you can afford to be charitable?

17. How valuable is your time? What's more important: to have any job or to have a job you enjoy?

18. Where do morals come from? Philosophy? Religion? Science? Psychology? Politics?

19. Is everyone worthy of compassion? Is there such a thing as evil or do criminals simply have bad brains?

20. If sexuality is a choice, when did you choose yours? Could you choose otherwise? What's more potent, nature or nurture? Which affected you more?

21. If you could start again, would you choose a bohemian lifestyle? Or is stoicism for you?

22. When you die, what legacy will you leave? Does a legacy even matter after you're dead?

23. What would happen if you acted, dressed and ate differently? Do you have good reasons to change? Do you have good reasons to stay the same?

24. Starting with a blank slate, what would your life look like if you, acting consciously, designed it? What could you change today that would be in alignment with that design?

I could go on and on with these questions but I'll keep it to these twenty-four to get your mind mulling. I want you to ask yourself where those ideas came from. Have you thought it through or are you parroting what you've heard in the past? You cannot find alignment in word, thought and deed if you don't know what you believe and why. I caution you to take your time with this exercise and make sure you are not merely succumbing to repeating what you've been taught. Make no mistake, we are all indoctrinated one way or another.

Do the introspective thing.

Dig Up the Roots of Your Truth Part II

Some people tend to commit to the first thing they hear or read and refuse to deviate. A very nice fellow would often go out of his way to question me about my beliefs (in my post-Christian phase). He would pose a question and I would answer. After a short time, it was apparent I'd read the Bible and he had not. This was a man who believed so deeply that he thought the Earth was only 6,000 years old. When he asserted this, I said, "That's interesting. That's roughly when the Sumerians invented glue." He replied, "That's interesting, but it's only if you believe in carbon dating." I asked what he knew of carbon dating. "Nothing," he admitted. "I just don't believe it can be accurate."

Scientific research demonstrates how stubborn people are about changing their minds in light of new information. It is a dangerous inertia that affects many societal institutions. Many are committed to the demonstrably false because admitting the truth would mean they were wrong before they accepted what's right. It's terrifying how difficult it can be to change people's minds, even when presented with solid evidence.

If you believe without knowing why you believe, you aren't a person. You are a recording. Your skull is a box filled with whatever somebody tossed into it. Be a person. Believe what you want but give it some thought so you know what and why you believe. I am arguing here for people to make conscious choices. If you are under stress and your approach to life management is passive, you won't be managing much.

The catch is, a passive choice is still a choice. You are not really passive. You are an agent of choice and thought. Not choosing to bowl on Friday nights is choosing to stay home. When you know what you think and why, you can then align your choices in thought, word and deed. When we let life happen to us, we fail to make these choices consciously. Without conscious choice, we waste time and effort. The cost of our illusions is regret.

People can defy their programming. I once belonged to a fundamentalist church. I'm now an atheist. (If you jumped to judging me harshly just then, reread your Bible and keep your stone casting to yourself.) In university someone told me I wasn't funny. I believed them until I had a couple of experiences that allowed me to entertain a new belief about myself. I went on to entertain others professionally.

I know. I'm not being funny in this chapter. That kind of felt like I was haranguing you, didn't it? Sorry about that.

Do the thing that defies unconscious programming that does not serve you or others.

To Be or Not To Be

Typically, when someone says they want to "get in touch" with themselves through meditation, I'm not sure what they mean or what they think they mean. Introspection often seems to accompany blurred communication or fuzzy thinking that sounds flaky to those who don't share the experience.

We're going to go deeper into this in a moment in an exercise I think you'll find stimulating. First, to illustrate why knowing yourself is so important (and not flaky and strange, at all) I want to tell you about a couple of suicides.

A friend from high school killed himself. He was a great loss. Kind, sweet and a talented young filmmaker, he hung himself at the age of seventeen. He was not allowed to see his girlfriend and he overreacted. There were many issues involved but his choice to end his young life always struck me as a fundamental error in understanding. If she was the love of his life, he could have waited a night. There would have been other girlfriends. I don't mean to sound glib or callous. Mental health problems are not so simple. Still, he had become fixated on one option. He saw suicide as his only choice.

Another suicide was that of a man of my acquaintance. He was a sharp young man who hated his job. Time away from work did not make his problems go away. Friends told him to quit. He could have done many things, not the least of which would have been to choose unemployment. (He had a very bad job.) Instead, he killed himself in a gruesome way. All his other choices were rendered meaningless when he acted on that suicidal impulse.

This is what philosopher Jean-Paul Sartre called Bad Faith. According to Sartre, we are free with a wide range of possibilities to choose from. When we limit our freedom by insisting life must be one way, we are in Bad Faith. I would call this state Unaligned. The filmmaker and the prison guard were so out of alignment and so committed to one course, stress killed them. Sadly, if they'd studied Sartre, perhaps these young men would have been more open to other possibilities.

I am not discounting the power of depression here. It is a mistake to say that suicides happen simply because people aren't happy. It's much more complex than that. Neurochemical imbalances are involved. However, I'm convinced that narrow choices lead to more stress and possibly depression. This might be a chicken or egg distinction, but the road back to mental health is paved with more choices.

Yes, depression sucks and depression kills. Brain chemical imbalances need to be addressed by professionals. Helping hands, not accusations, must be extended to those in need. Our pain is not all about the circumstances in which we find ourselves but also about the state of our brains.

To get out of trouble, we have to make change on all levels: thought, word, deed (and often pharmaceutically.) If you're thinking about hurting yourself or others, you need help. Pick up the phone. Dial 911.

**Do the kind thing,
for yourself and others.**

**For suicide prevention, awareness and support,
you'll find hotlines worldwide at
Suicide.org.**

Let Go of All or Nothing Part I

To make big changes in your life, you have to make a lot of small changes consistently. A lot of people burn out when they try to do too much at once. That's why I ask you to treat this book as a buffet. Take what you can use, implement what you can and leave what doesn't work for you.

The mindset that is sure to make you stumble when making life changes is all or nothing thinking. We'll blow one meal and then decide to dump the whole diet for the rest of the day. We'll break a streak of success and delay starting the next streak.

This is self-sabotage and it doesn't make a lot of sense. It comes from a pass/fail view of the game. Instead, I suggest you look upon the challenges you set for yourself as a process. Instead of thinking of nutrition as on a diet or off, think of it simply as trying to eat healthier. There's no bandwagon to fall off of. You're simply making the best choices you can *most* of the time. When you don't make the best choices, you don't write yourself off forever.

Think of all your efforts as a process and you minimize losses instead of giving up and maximizing them.

Do the thing that minimizes setbacks.

Let Go of All or Nothing Part II

In one of my stress management classes, I noticed someone in the front row was growing visibly agitated as I spoke. She fidgeted and shifted in her seat. The rest of the class was with me but I could tell I had said something that drove her to distraction. Finally, she burst out with, "I have a five-year-old! I can't do all this!"

"What could you make time to do?" I asked.

"Nothing!"

"You can't choose to do one thing to help yourself and give yourself and your five-year-old more energy?"

"You don't understand. I'm really busy."

"Then, I'm sorry, but I really can't imagine how I can help you."

She smiled in triumph. She didn't want to manage her stress and she wasn't willing to change anything. She wanted someone to acknowledge that she was stressed out, helpless and hopeless. That was not the thrust of my speech in a stress management class, of course, but I guess that's what that participant thought she needed. After I agreed with her that she faced time management challenges, she was more willing to hear what else I had to say.

Every week I suggest remedial exercise or make some suggestion to a client to reduce their pain, increase energy and reduce their stress. The vast majority of the time those suggestions are welcome. (They're coming to me, after all. I'm not chasing people down the street and screaming at them about their posture.) When my expertise is unwelcome, though, I do not check out.

Whether my suggestions will help everyone or not, the thing I try to do is remain present, stay ready to adapt and I hold on to calm. I listen very carefully. When I work, my mind is not elsewhere. I am focused on the health and happiness of each client. I'm watchful for body language and subtle cues that my client and I are not in alignment. When I'm serene so are my clients.

I wrote before of the client who said she was too busy to take a deep breath. You can't help everyone and not all therapies or every therapist is for everyone. However, my message in this chapter is for the helpers. Let go of insisting on being right. Listen first. If you nod when people speak, they relax, open up more and they're encouraged.

Talk less. Understand more. Relate to each person as they want to be related to. This is the essence of gathering information and communicating that you care. They'll know you still care even if they disagree with you.

Do the caring thing.

Objectivity

Most of the time, we already know what we need to do to manage our lives better. Maybe we don't want to risk change. Perhaps we don't have the time or energy for the effort or we're scared to begin in case we fail. We tell ourselves there must be some secret that only successful people know. We tell ourselves that anyone who is managing their lives better must be luckier. We tell ourselves that other people must have more time than we do.

Each day has twenty-four hours.
That applies to everyone.

We want shortcuts. There are ways to do things better and faster, yes, but very few means to success are the sort of tactics that allow you to "set it and forget it."

If you know what you should do already, why haven't you done it by now? Because it's hard? It is hard to change and it's hard to stay changed. Course correction takes a lot of small movements over a long time.

I think it was Tony Robbins who used the analogy of driving a car. As you drive, you make a lot of small movements of the steering wheel to stay in your lane and get to the destination. That's what every day is like on the road to change. It's a lot of little changes made consistently so you don't wind up in the ditch.

If you're having a difficult time connecting with the knowledge you already have, try treating your most stressful problems more objectively. If a friend came to you asking for honest advice about the same issues, what would you tell them?

For ourselves, we come up with rationalizations and excuses. For others, we're much clearer.

We tell ourselves, "But I like chocolate." We tell others, "Eat a salad every day."

We tell ourselves, "I'll catch up someday." We tell others, "Not if you don't start now."

We tell ourselves, "I'll plan a vacation when I clear off everything else I need to do." We tell others, "You know that's never going to happen, right?"

We tell ourselves, "But I love him." We tell others, "You can do better."

We tell ourselves, "If I ask for help, people will think I'm stupid." We tell others, "C'mon, man! Not asking for help when you need it is stupid."

Do the objective thing.

Better days

Once upon a time, I worked with an older gentleman who waxed nostalgic about his senior year in high school. He was a very accomplished fellow but, to hear him tell it, his best days were far behind him. Despite a great marriage, having children, becoming wealthy and being in great shape, he looked in the far past for the best year of his life.

Let's pause to think about that for a moment. Is it just me that finds this notion repulsive? It's good to have memories of good times. However, if I thought all my best times were far behind me I'm sure I'd go to bed, pull the covers over my head and never leave. To better manage our stress we have to have goals and ways to make those goals into a reality. We need events to look forward to. These goals need not be on the scale of trips around the world on an annual basis. I'm talking about social outings with friends, good conversation and doing the things you want to do.

A life with more such events has more milestones. With more milestones, we have anchors to our memories. You probably don't remember all the grocery stores you have visited. Grocery store visits rarely qualify as life events unless shots are fired, you meet a celebrity or you win a shopping spree. When you experience more, life is richer because you are more *engaged* with what you are doing.

I have an excellent sense of time passing. I can't explain the mechanism but it's a strange and fairly useless little superpower. When I wake up each morning, before I open my eyes, I guess what time it is. Invariably, when I look at the clock I'm precise within two or three minutes at most. However, I've noticed that when you lose track of time, it's a good sign that you're fully engaged in what you're doing. When I worked in retail, I always knew what time it was and it seemed the clock hands were spinning counterclockwise.

Days filled with drudgery are a stress. When one day looks too much like all the others, you endure the stress of a life that feels long because it's boring. We don't want boring. To elude boredom and add value to our lives, we must embrace opportunities to change. We must risk and engage and find the fun.

When you are engaged in what you are doing and paying attention, your relationship to time changes. For instance, one day I traveled with friends to visit the Toronto Zoo. On the way back, we got into a car accident. I remember the shift as the accident appeared to happen in slow motion. Near death experiences really make you pay attention.

Fortunately, nobody died. I escaped with some harsh bruises from the seat belt. That night, I attended a party with other friends. I recounted my narrow escape and felt very grateful to be alive and unhurt.

Late that night, sitting on the front step of my friend's house, I looked back on the day with a sense of wonder. It was not all pleasant, of course, but that was one of the longest days of my life. Time slowed. Confronting mortality can do that, I guess. I recalled everything in such minute detail. My senses were momentarily heightened but, more important and long-lasting was the awareness that making memories and having milestones is important to happiness.

Soon I will take a trip with my family that we can only barely afford at the moment. However, the kids are growing up and my daughter will be in university far away this time next year. This may be our last chance to have a family vacation where it's just us together, making memories. My wife and I have decided that money comes and goes but memories last. We'll make it work. Life is too short. With engagement we make more memories. A life with lots of rich memories feels longer (in a pleasant way.)

Do things (things you want to do).
For a full life, fill it with events.

Experiential Exercise

Have a meal that you have never before experienced. Go to an ethnic restaurant that is totally unfamiliar to you. We tend to eat the same few meals over and over. Change your experience and you might even enjoy expanding your palate.

Take a risk on something you're not sure you'll like.

Suggestions:

Rent a ride in a hot air balloon.

Have a pot luck get-together where everyone brings something exotic with ingredients they've never tried before.

Try hot yoga.

Volunteer at a senior's center, veteran's center or food bank.

Build something.

Create something.

Take music lessons.

Travel to the place you've always wanted to travel.

**Do the thing
you've always wanted to do.**

It's Not Too Late

A friend of mine who was approaching 50 decided to learn Portuguese. It's not an easy language to learn but my friend dedicated himself to the task.

The toughest thing about learning a new language is that, while you're learning, you sound like an idiot. (Read David Sedaris on learning French in *Me Talk Pretty One Day* for hilarious examples.) Anyone who learns a language later in life has to let go of being self-conscious. It takes more bravery than it does intelligence.

After diligent study, my friend learned enough Portuguese for stilted, struggling and embarrassing conversations with Brazilians. Then he became so fluent he made a business presentation to the Brazilian ambassador to Canada. He owns several businesses in Brazil now, no translators needed. No more embarrassment.

The same engagement with life, love of people and enthusiasm for travel led my friend to become a shipping magnate. He wasn't a shipping magnate before he developed his interests. His success sprang from the person he chose to be.

The doctor who delivered me died of cancer. Even when he became bedridden, he was teaching himself French. There's a sadness in that, but power, too. Cancer didn't stop him from being curious about the world and engaged with life to the end.

There are many such interested, interesting, inspired and engaged people. I think we need to make a lot more such people, don't you?

Inspiration is everywhere if you look. Try watching the movie *Under the Tuscan Sun* or read *Eat, Pray, Love*. Watch and read anything that inspires you. See it and read it and do so again.

For me, *Rocky, The Karate Kid, The Princess Bride* and *Finding Forrester* are inspiring. Anything done well can inspire. When I saw the colossal architecture of the Peace Palace in The Hague, I was moved to tears by the achievement.

Encouraging, enthusiastic and aspiring people inspire. Find them and hang out with them. People who ask why too much can suck your energy and inspiration away.

Director Kevin Smith suggests you make friends with people who ask why not? Why Not people don't say no to new ideas and opportunities.

"I want to make a movie."

"Sure! You could do that! Why not?"

"Do you want to be in my movie?"

"Sure! Why not?"

Don't just make friends with Why Not people. Become one of them.

Do the thing you're scared to do.

Facing Illness

Much of this book focuses on things you can control. (Remember? Don't worry about what you can't control.) But what if the situation is more dire? Organizing your day and decluttering your office are useful things but much less so in the face of a scary diagnosis from your doctor. When facing surgery and mortality, what then?

If this is your situation, call in backup. You need a support system. This is where having friends and family can be so helpful. However, for any illness, there are support organizations.

I know someone who is facing dire health challenges. He lives in the remote desert. Still, between travel and the internet and family support, he has made many allies in the fight for his life.

If you're facing a life and death situation, you will certainly find it useful to connect with people who have already traveled the road you're on. Talk to support workers. Work with your doctors and do what needs to be done. Don't succumb to pessimism.

A friend of mine was diagnosed with a twenty-five pound tumor. Think of that. Twenty-five pounds! It turned out to be benign. She's fine now. It sure was scary, though.

Obsessing over your symptoms increases your stress. It can increase pain, your respiration rate, interfere with your sleep and increase your blood pressure, too. Manage illness. Do not identify with it. Oncologists tell their patients to refer to the illness as, "the cancer," not "my cancer." The illness does not define you.

Illness is a ride. There are ups and downs but you don't get to exit the ride until it's done. To get to the other end of trouble, make plans, make allies and connect with others. If you are dealing with the end of life, the challenges are similar and the strategies to deal with the stress are the same.

I'm struck by the poignancy of Christopher Hitchens's thoughts on undergoing cancer treatment. The author said that people encouraged him to fight but chemotherapy is a passive process. He didn't feel like a fighter. He understood that people meant well but framing his end-of-life struggles that way added to his stress. Instead, as is evident from a video recording of his last book signing party, he seemed determined to enjoy the company of others. The love shone through.

Some people suffer mean thoughts about themselves at the end of life. They may be angry or die in regret. It seems the only way to temper the sadness is not to live a life you'll regret. Stress management is life management, so we all have the tools to work on that goal.

Before we move on, let me share a pet peeve of mine. I hate obituaries that use phrases like, "after a brave battle, So-and-so succumbed...." No. So-and-so did not lose his or her battle. They died as we all must. Accepting the "lost the battle" framing makes every death a defeat. Not fair, is it? Not in a game in which everyone eventually loses no matter what. Better that we celebrate the lives of the dead. Best that we make lives we would be proud to celebrate.

More than anything, terminally ill patients need patience. Setbacks, fear, anger and death are all natural and to be expected. Make sure you get your full serving of joy and laughter, too. Grab it while you can.

When I was a child, the prospect of being condemned to hell terrified me. A lot of people would call that propaganda and child abuse now. A vindictive god that would send a little boy to fire and brimstone haunted my thoughts. Then I happened to watch an episode of an old TV show called *Room 222*.

Room 222 was about a history teacher trying to make a difference with high school kids. (I had such a crush on Karen Valentine!) When a student died, one student tells the others something like, "If you spend your whole life worrying about death, you're dead already." That one line was enough to change my outlook forever.

We are all in pursuit of a good death. Aside from pain management issues, a good death is really about having lived a good life. Let's focus on that.

Focus on now.

Focus on the variables we can control.

Connect with others.

Make friends while there's still time.

Make a difference in people's lives while there is still time.

Laugh more and make others laugh more.

As much as you can, enjoy the ride.

You're still alive so do the life-affirming things.

Support in the Face of Illness

One of the most significant components to happiness is social support. There are plenty of ways to find it. Most people will find their support among family and friends. Unfortunately, not all family and friends will necessarily be supportive in times of need. Select your allies carefully. Unless you want your personal business spread hither and yon, don't consult the town gossip. Not everyone is blessed with compassion, insight, and understanding of your situation.

When you share information with others, be clear about boundaries. Who else may know about your life situation and concerns? Be particularly cautious when sharing information across social media. You may not want the details of your personal life bleeding over from an instant message thread to a post to the public. That could add to your stress without incurring further benefit.

Beyond the family and friends, there are many support groups for whatever life challenge you are dealing with. If you are in a rural area your number of choices may be limited. However, there are online support groups for just about any concern. By listening to the experiences of others, what they faced and how they succeeded in managing their stress, strangers across the world can become friends who support one another.

Another option is to form your own mastermind group to deal with your illness. Gather like-minded individuals who face the same worries and who are seeking solutions. With any support group, have a moderator in place who monitors the group and keeps them on track. For these groups to work well, rules of confidentiality must be in place. Online or in person, each individual in the group must bear the purpose of the gathering in mind. While it can be useful for people to vent, that is not all a support group should be.

A friend of mine with multiple sclerosis was plugged into a vast social network of fellow sufferers. As a health care practitioner, as well, she was an expert in the subject. She took phone calls from people with questions and concerns. She allowed them to vent about their frustrations, too, of course. However, she did not allow the venting to go on too long. She even set a timer for five minutes. After five minutes, her rule was to pivot to conversation oriented to solutions or management.

She accomplished this diplomatically. She was never without compassion but she was an excellent facilitator and patient advocate. She never allowed an individual or group to get bogged down in despair.

You may find solutions to whatever stresses you at your local church, the people with whom you play basketball or at a formal community group like Al-Anon or AA. Maybe you are the mastermind of your mastermind group. In any case, find a mentor, sympathetic voices and people in search of solutions.

Not all solutions are for everyone, of course, but what all successful support strategies have in common is social connection. We are social animals. We do better facing challenges when we don't try to face them alone.

When I was very young I had a fantasy that when I became successful I would have no one to thank. I would owe nothing. That was stupid pride. No success is accomplished alone.

Suggestions:

1. Plug into a group for social support and choose your allies carefully.

2. Keep swinging the focus from negative to positive.

3. Find accountability partners to report to.

4. Expect to give support, not just receive it.

5. Remember that you are not alone.

Do the social thing.

Our Irrational Expectations

Don't expect irrational people to be rational.

This is the key stress management tool which will help you maintain perspective when encountering unreasonable people. People are emotional animals. I don't mean animals in a bad way at all. It's just that we are affected by our glands. Our cognitive functions are sometimes impaired by those gland secretions. If you don't believe me, think of all the times you were attracted to someone who would be terrible for you in every way but sexually. Yeah. I know, right? End of argument.

Even intelligent people have blindspots. We're all incredibly ignorant about something but, be it pride or misplaced confidence, we often feel compelled to have instant opinions about everything.

Everybody is irrational about something sometimes. No one is an expert on everything. We can screw up, forgive and let go of regret. That's not the same as dealing with pathological liars, rude people and those determined to stay obnoxious and ignorant.

"But!" someone is yelling again. "What about compassion? We're supposed to feel compassion for everyone!"

If you're a martyr or a saint who believes in unlimited compassion, rude irrational people will exhaust you. Focus your energies on your tribe. Don't sacrifice yourself on the alter of compassion. You will reach burnout and then you'll be of no use to anyone. Energy is not unlimited. Spend it wisely.

Do the rational thing.

Gratitude

Thank someone. This was brought home to me in a strong and sad way last year. I had taken some time off from massage therapy to devote myself to writing. When I came back to work at my old clinic, I didn't have the same clientele anymore. One of my old clients did come back, a financial wizard who was one of the happiest and most successful people I've ever known.

On the table, he was a talker, always quick with a joke. We bounced jokes off each other. After his last session, I was doing the exit interview, wrapping things up to see how he'd reacted to treatment. I don't know what made me say so but, at the door, I paused to tell him something I'd never said to a patient. I felt awkward saying it and he probably felt a little awkward hearing it. However, our unease soon dissipated. I plunged in, not knowing why. "I'm not supposed to have favorites but, man, I'm so glad you're back! When I see you're on my schedule, I know it's going to be a good day. Thanks so much for being a regular client again. I really appreciate you."

He laughed and smiled and clapped me on the shoulder. We shook hands and said goodbye, sure to see each other again soon for another appointment. I never saw him alive again. A few weeks later, he died of a heart attack at 53. He literally dropped dead. He appeared to be one of the fittest men I knew in his age bracket. His family genetics worked against him.

I'd known him for years and I was devastated by the loss. I dedicated one of my books to him, for what that's worth. I still miss him and I think the world is a little darker without his presence. Still, it does make me feel a little better that I acted on the impulse to have an earnest moment. Basically, I thanked him for being in my life and I thanked him for being him. I suggest you thank someone, too, before it's too late. You never know, when you won't be able to tell the important people in your life what they mean to you. Good things left unsaid are stressors we can do without.

My friend the pastor was big on praising people when he caught them doing something right. Speaking of praise, he said, "Send them their flowers while they're alive! They can't enjoy them after they're dead! They aren't sticking around for the eulogy!"

Do the thankful thing.

The Selfish Thing

A friend of mine was in terrible shape. He'd survived serious surgery and chemo was next. His prognosis was not good. He had a young family at home and he'd shed a lot of what he called, "midnight tears." Of all tears, midnight tears are the loneliest. That's when you weep alone and feel sorry for yourself.

You know what my friend did to feel better? He looked for ways to make the guy in the next hospital bed feel better. We give because it feels good to give. There's a reward system in our brains that provides a natural pharmacy of happy drugs made by the body. Generosity of spirit is a joy that the selfish wall off from themselves. In helping others, we are helped. We assert our power, knowing that the powerless suffer more stress. You really do get when you give.

One of the things I like to do when I'm out and about is to buy the homeless a cookie or a coffee. For the price of a cup of coffee, you get to feel really good. It feels so good, a cynic might even call it a selfish act.

Do the selfish thing and give.

Take Time to Dance

In *Time on Fire: My Comedy of Terrors*, actor Evan Handler recounts his journey back from a dire life-threatening diagnosis. Handler manages to make his true story both heartfelt and funny. One of the scenes that has stuck with me is Handler hooked up to an IV pole and, weakly, making it to his hospital room window to dance. His nurse wasn't even sure what he was doing. He had to tell her he was dancing.

If he can do it under those circumstances, most of us can. Put on whatever music that energizes you and let yourself get into it. If you can't stand to dance, sit and dance in your chair. If someone catches you dancing, invite them to join you and look at them weird if they don't.

We don't dance enough. Blow off some steam daily.

Do the dancing thing.

Money Matters

**Money represents energy and security.
Money management is stress and energy
management.**

Do the things that matter.

Stress Management is for Everyone

Many of the suggestions in this book are geared to entrepreneurs, white collar workers, freelancers and people who tend to have more control over their work environments. Naturally, if you run your own company, stress management strategies are easier to implement. You're the boss.

White collar workers tend to have financial strategies in place. I won't delve deeply into financial wizardry since I'm not a financial wizard. If you don't have savings and a retirement plan set up already, the perfect time to arrange that was in your early twenties. The next best time is immediately. Consult a finance professional. As a financial genius I know once told me, "No matter what you do about your financial future, it's essential you do something."

But what if you aren't the boss? Most stress-busting books don't address money management issues. Implementing winning life hacks can be harder to implement for employees and the unemployed. Most stress management guides do not address the problems that disenfranchised groups suffer.

In psychological terms, those in the lower socio-economic strata are called, "at risk." This is shorthand for anyone who has fewer advantages, less money and less support. In short, those "at risk" are those who have less power. They are too often ignored.

As I write this, the middle class is shrinking. The rumor is that North America has recovered or is recovering from the recession that began in 2008. That's not true where I live. My part of the country is still largely in a recession. Wall Street has recovered. Main Street has not. If you don't have enough money to make the rent, how do you manage stress?

More people are becoming employed in the so-called Gig Economy, where customers expect more for less. Uber and Fiverr, for instance, are solutions for some people desperate for work. These companies are also symbolic of a problem. The world has moved on from job security. Many people no longer have the option of working for one company all their lives. They aren't looking forward to a comfortable pension and they don't have enough savings for retirement.

The next chapter is one of the longest in this book. It's about managing your stress when you don't have much money to manage. If you don't have much money, have compassion for yourself. Don't skip it.

Do the thing for your future.

Stress Management on a Budget

As someone who has often lived hand-to-mouth, I have a few suggestions for stress management on a tight budget:

1. Get professional help. Consult a reputable credit counsellor. A friend of mine was under incredible stress over her finances. Her money situation had collapsed for a lot of reasons but it turned out the way forward was simple. After getting her accounts assessed, she was told she could declare bankruptcy. That's not the answer for everyone, of course, but it was a revelation to my friend. A great weight was lifted from her shoulders and she is no longer dangerously stressed. A fresh start has her back in control and she's a much happier person now.

2. Pay down debt. Credit card interest is usurious. There is a time to accrue debt. It shouldn't be a way of life. If it is, you'll be under more stress. Leave your credit card at home. Don't use it unless it's an emergency. Avoid Payday loans and similar schemes that trap people in debt.

3. Dump luxuries you can't afford. This is often an issue for people who were once paid well but find themselves without a job. Once you attain an income where you can afford the full satellite package and the latest smartphone, you're more reluctant to economize. This sense of entitlement can hamper your efforts to recover. This is especially tough when your kid is hoping for the latest game console for his birthday and you're struggling to pay bills. (I've been there.)

Be honest with your children. Tell them when you can't afford expensive gifts. Pretending hurts you and will hurt them. Don't add to the spiral of debt. Find more affordable gifts and other ways to celebrate. This is difficult, I know. Each Christmas many people go deeper in debt and some may never recover.

Holiday seasons are a good time to focus on social interaction. You won't see this issue discussed anywhere because there is so much pressure to turn holidays into consumer frenzies. It may help you to consider that the rush we get from buying, giving and receiving things is kind of like a lot of addictions: we chase a quick high but usually receive little to no long-term benefit.

4. Your income is not what you make. It's what you keep.

I know several proud freelancers who would refuse to work a side job for a salary. However, as their tiny enterprises limp along, employees on salary are actually making more money than the stubborn business guy who wants to remain independent of a boss. (I know. I've been that stubborn business guy who has problems with authority.)

Look at your spreadsheets objectively and honestly. Perseverance is great. So is knowing when to quit and when to try switching to something that pays. One of the reasons I took multiple jobs was to finance expansion of my main business. There is no shame in taking a side hustle.

5. Can you afford to move to where the jobs are? Too many people focus on their income without paying any attention to the outgo. You can make what sounds like a lot of money and still be desperately poor if you live in New York City. The same income with a lower cost of living elsewhere might make you debt-free in short order.

6. If your income is low, most financial information you hear in the media is not aimed at you.

When I reached a certain age I thought I should have investments in the stock market. Smart people told me so but they were smart people with more money. It was good advice for them but terrible advice for me.

Very little advice in popular media is aimed at the poor. Financial advisors are selling services and products the poor can't afford. It's unfortunate, but it's probably not a conspiracy. Similarly, *Consumer Reports* will tell you which are the best and safest cars on the road. They aren't telling you how you can afford to buy the best and safest.

The shift in the economy was reflected on television, particularly with changes to home renovation programming. When such shows first became popular, the premise was usually, "Watch how we do this kitchen reno for a mere $50,000." As the economy tanked, more television became geared to cheap paint jobs to increase curb appeal, selling houses and redecorating living rooms for $1000 (or $100 or pillows they could find at a yard sale.)

Find the advisors who give you advice that is appropriate to your income.

7. Consume less and avoid spending money you don't have. Use your debit card or cash instead of your credit card. This strategy requires you pay more attention to your bank balance, but you'll pay less to credit card companies this way.

8. Ask yourself, are you a consumer or a producer? The world wants you to be a consumer. Shop. Buy. Eat. Use. Throw away. Repeat. That's the subtext of every commercial. The propaganda is constant on every screen and sign.

Research varies widely, but you may be exposed to 300 to 700 marketing messages each day. You are probably exposed to far more than that but human nervous systems rarely process more than that. It's still sensory overload and it's all geared to getting you to buy something.

**For more on this,
check out the chapter titled:
*Combat Sensory Overload.***

Defy societal programming that wants you to buy, buy, buy! Become a producer instead. Sell and earn. Sell and earn more than you buy.

9. Watch what and where you buy. My wife's most expensive leather jacket, probably originally priced at a few hundred dollars. She found it at a discount store for a few dollars. That coat looks like a million bucks on her.

10. If you're poor, dump your shame. This section is about to get political, but social change for everyone's benefit requires individual responsibility, a conscience and political action.

There's a war on the poor and it is unconscionable. Poverty is unfortunate but it is in the condemnation of low income people where the real shame lies.

There are far too many variables that contribute to poverty. Many of those variables are systemic failures. It is tempting to say that the best thing you can do for the poor is not be one of them. That statement would have more power if the poor were given more opportunities to raise their socioeconomic status.

The phrase, "pull yourself up by your boot straps," was originally an ironic statement meant to point out the absurdity of defying gravity that way. It has come to be a slogan that symbolizes a lack of compassion. It is too often uttered by people who do not appreciate the difficulties of others. Disadvantaged people do not have bootstraps.

If you make minimum wage or more, advocate for others to make more, too. Sometimes people above the poverty line work to keep others down instead of lifting everyone up. Everyone deserves a decent life.

Often the poorest people are working harder than the wealthy few. Worse, despite the fact that his or her income is eighty times higher, a CEO cannot work eighty times harder than the company's lowest-paid employee. Wage disparity is shameful.

Oddly enough, cities that have enacted higher minimum wages are experiencing greater prosperity. Despite dire predictions to the contrary, having a conscience makes economic sense for everyone. The facts are on the side of the worker. When we pay people a decent wage, they have the power to buy what companies sell. Instead of cutting work forces to the bone, we must increase buying power. Buying power, not more unemployment, is the engine of capitalism.

Because of lobbyists and the money it takes to get elected, political power is often not on the side of the worker. For instance, Walmart is, as of this writing, the biggest company in the world. Their financial success is supported not just by consumers, but by taxpayers. Walmart typically pays their employees so little that government programs subsidize the company. These welfare programs should be for the benefit of the unemployed. Instead, tax dollars support a corporation that can afford to pay its employees but chooses not to.

Now you know why you'll never see this book for sale on the shelves at Walmart.

11. Gather resources and allies around you. Food banks and community gardens in urban areas are two such resources. When you are not opting out of needless consumerism, buy local whenever possible. Dollars spent in your community are spent again many times over. Dollars spent in a big box store are sent away and they don't come back.

12. An educated society is a safer and more stable society. Higher education is a way out of poverty but formal post-secondary education is not available to everyone, everywhere. Your choices are more complex than they once were.

Investing in your education may be the best investment you'll ever make. It could also lead to no job when you're done and more debt you can't escape. University used to be the solution — and a relatively inexpensive one — to every financial problem. Now, for many, it's another problem. A sign of the times is that some American students are studying abroad in countries where university education is provided free.

Evaluate carefully what you could study that has a good record of job placement post-graduation. If that's not an option, look at other ways to better your situation. Between libraries and online options, educational opportunities abound that do not necessitate huge gambles on tuition and student debt that does not end.

13. Everyone has something they are good at that can be monetized. Find your passion. Discover the angle. Find a way. My elders told me there's no way to make money playing video games. Then my generation went on to design games that make more than the movie industry.

Some of my son's generation are making money off others watching them play video games. Don't get caught up in the inertia of old concepts. Figure out what you can do and make it happen. Gather with likeminded people so you can help each other achieve common goals.

It's common wisdom to mock artistic creatives. Then those same people spouting common wisdom will watch TV, play video games each night and see a movie every weekend. Watch where the money goes and get in on the supply end of what it buys (not what it used to buy).

14. You don't have to be a millionaire to be successful. It's a sad cliche, but plenty of millionaires are consistently unhappy before and after they make their millions. They are still people, after all.

It is unfortunate that the American dream has been so influenced by reality TV (or maybe we should call it unreality TV). The American dream was once much less ambitious and people did not judge their success or failure by a few outliers. People wanted one vacation a year, a home they could someday own and they wanted to work enough to be comfortable. It was a simple, middle class goal that was more achievable in the post-war boom of the fifties.

Stress management is little more than successful life management. Lots of books will tell you to work hard to reach for the brass ring. I'm telling you I'll still love you if you're ordinary.

My grandmother was the poor wife of a Baptist preacher. I loved her because she fixed the string on my first bow. I loved her because she made biscuits with too much salt and butter. I loved her for the aromas that emanated from the pantry in her old house. I loved her because she was my grandmother.

Everyone will still love you if you're ordinary because, in some way, you remain extraordinary. Everyone has something to give. Everyone has something to sell. You may not have the coin but everyone has value.

15. Find mentors and emulate examples that are relevant to your situation.

When I turned twenty-two, I had just graduated from university. I'd moved to Toronto and money was tight. I was living in boarding houses with a lot of cockroaches and stuffing newspapers in the heels of my shoes to make them last longer.

My father (trying to be helpful) said, "By the time I was your age, I had a business, a wife, a house, two kids and two cars." He was from a different time. It was an economic boom time. His situation was irrelevant to mine.

Who do you know who is finding their way out of their financial stress *now*? Follow them.

16. Don't waste time envying anyone.

Recently, my father regaled me with an update about an old classmate who has become fabulously wealthy. I remember that guy. He was, pardon my honesty, an asshole. Maybe he's not now so I won't cast further aspersions. I will say I don't want to be him. In all the universe, there's only one me and I still think that's pretty special no matter how many zeroes are in my bank account.

Money does not equal success. Money can equal power and security, but mostly, money equals money. It can help people be better off but having it doesn't make anyone a better person. You need a minimum amount of resources to manage your stress. Beware of thinking there is no maximum amount of money that will ease your way.

17. The media is full of propaganda that tells you to have it all or you're nothing. Don't fall for it.

Mainstream media sometimes divides the population into makers and takers. It's not true. Look more carefully at those makers and you will find a different story. You'll find many of the rich routinely evade taxes with fictitious home offices in tax havens like the Cayman Islands. You'll find corporate welfare queens that suck more money from taxpayers than any disadvantaged person could imagine doing.

I'm not saying that we should eat the rich. I would suggest however that Henry Ford understood a fundamental principal of capitalism: pay your workers enough so they can participate in the economy. With low wages, workers cannot also be customers. Let's keep it real about who drives economies off cliffs. It's the people gambling with our economic future. It's not the poor and teachers' unions that hurt the economy in 2008. It was Wall Street, unregulated greed and predatory banking.

People living at sustenance levels are not responsible for the economic collapse. Don't aspire to count yourself among the greedy. We don't need to be greedy to manage our stress. We can do good to do well.

18. Be objective about the numbers you're currently working with. Write them down. Figure out what you can spend, how much you can save and, if possible, what to invest.

My wife and I have a policy we enacted long ago. We never talk about money late in the evening. Questions we can't immediately answer would keep us up at night when we should be sleeping.

In the cold light of day, without passion, anger or worry, we make our plans and do what we can.

**Do the things about money that you can.
Anything that is out of your control is not for you to
worry about.**

Price & Value

Before you can complete the exercise in the next chapter, there's something you need to know about what you charge for your work:

1. The price must cover your costs plus profit. Aside from loss leaders and temporary discounts, if your regular price cannot cover your costs and make a profit, your product or service is not viable.

2. The fee you charge has nothing to do with your perception of the worth of the product or service.

3. The fee you charge has everything to do with the *value* your buyers place upon it. That doesn't seem fair to you, does it? It is fair to the customer.

I know someone who is trying to sell a property. They've been at it for a long time. It's a large, beautiful piece of land with a creek and a house big enough to be a B&B. It's a property with a lot going for it for the right buyer.

A couple of times a year, someone comes around to have a look at the place. They ooh and ah over this farm. Nobody buys and no one has even made an offer in years. The asking price is too high. "But," the owner objects, "it's worth the price I'm asking!"

If the prospective buyer is not willing to pay the price, that product or service is not worth that price. It doesn't matter what you paid for it. It doesn't matter what you consider just. You can only charge what the market will bear.

To somebody, I think this book will be worth millions of dollars. This book could save lives. Instead, you paid a few bucks for it. See? Commerce!

Never confuse an Ought with an Is. You can't change the world with wishes. You must see the world as it is and *then* take action.

Do the thing at the right price.

Make Money by the Calendar

Your calendar is your time machine. I touched on this before. Now that we're talking about money and making some, it's time to delve deeper. It is time to plot and plan the big stuff with less stress. Step into the time machine and let's figure out how to work backward from your goal.

Whatever your goal is, you can get there by working backward and making the steps actionable, realistic and easy to plug into your calendar. This is important, so I'm going to put this in a way that will appeal to people who hate math and cold calculations.

Here's a summary of what I mean by working backward from your goal:

1. You need a target. Make a statement. For instance, "I will create a new Mac app this year, market it and sell it."

2. Assume you've already hit your target. What does that look and feel like?

3. How much would it cost in time and energy? What do you have to learn to make this happen?

A friend of mine made Mac apps. He was a bill collector who hated his job. Starting from scratch, he bought a Mac and, by studying on his own, boned up on all the tech required to become a programmer.

Now that you know someone else did it, I hope the prospect of trying something new to you is less stressful.

4. Can you spend that time and energy?

5. Will you? How? Make a list.

6. Get out your calendar and start blocking out the time for each phase of your project. Put the elements of the list you made into your calendar.

Big projects are intimidating. It's overwhelming to take on a big goal. If this is your first ambitious project, you may have to start by cleaning up your office, making an office to clean up, or overhauling your life.

People can and do manage awe-inspiring makeovers of their lives. However, success stories in the media tell you a bit about the Before, a lot about the After and too little about the challenges of the in-between.

Before we get deeper into using the time machine, we need to discuss the Between briefly. Why? Because a sense of entitlement causes stress. I'm always on the lookout for origins of stress so I can eliminate the needless causes and manage the rest.

Entitlement is crippling. If you suffer this particular confusion between an Ought and an Is, we definitely need to address the Between before we use the time machine to its full effect.

Do the Between thing.

What is the Between?

The Between is the dash between the date of your birth and the date of your death. The Between is the struggle that nobody sees unless somebody makes a biopic of your life as a rockstar. The Between is the learning curve, the struggle, the training sequence and the montage that everyone glosses over when they think about success. The Between is hunkering down in the editing phase of this book and realizing you are about 48,000 words into a book with a deadline that's only a month away. (Heh. Yeah, that's me today, stuck in the Between.)

The Between is not the high points of awards ceremonies and laudatory podcast interviews. It's not the view that comes after all the hard work. It's not the fake-perfect Facebook version of your life that your online friends see. The Between is when you do the work. The Between only looks easy in retrospect.

The Between is getting up early to go to the gym even though it's cold. The Between is eating asparagus and kale shakes even when you're tired of eating for nutrition and want to eat for fun. The Between is *hard*.

After the work is done we see all the success and none of the failures. Disappointments and frustrations that littered the path to success are swept away when the payoffs roll in.

When people see all my books on sale, they see the product of a lot of Between. What they don't see is me writing for years, just for myself with no thought of selling my work. I just love writing, so that's what I did and do.

People don't see the low points of my Between. They didn't see the two years I took off from all other work to write. I did nothing else so sacrifices were made and not all the sacrifices were mine alone. People don't see that I went into debt to stay home and work while my wife worked ever harder and gave me an allowance of $60 a week.

They don't see me questioning myself and hating myself when my kids' friends went off on vacations we couldn't afford. When their classmates got yet another new cell phone and my kids had none, I resented those parents for spoiling their children. I wanted to spoil mine, too.

Yes, that was shitty of me, but that's how I felt: envious, selfish and angry. I thought life should be easier. That led to more stress. In my Between, I confused an Ought with an Is.

Don't ignore the Between. Expect it. Expect that, whatever your goal, it's probably going to be harder than you thought it might be. It's the expectation of easy achievement that sets people up for failure, stress, anxiety and depression. Obstacles are part of a successful process.

While it's true that you don't want to give yourself too much time, you have to keep it real. Tasks often take more time than you think, especially when you don't break projects down to their components. If you're still scaling the learning curve of how to do a thing, budget more time for the tasks involved. Success is not guaranteed. Only the Between is guaranteed.

How do you deal with the hard parts? Don't try to eat the elephant all at once. Break down your goals into smaller, achievable and short-term milestones. That's how you eat the elephant, one bite at a time. (But don't actually eat elephants. They are endangered.)

Bonus tip about the Between:

Watch *The Martian* with Matt Damon. I loved the audiobook performance and the book by Andy Weir. There is a great message in there about problem-solving. You deal with what's in front of you, one at a time. (Spoiler alert). Despite the odds piled high against you, *live.*

Now that we've gone to Mars and dealt with the Between, let's go deeper into the time machine. (Yes, I write science fiction, too.)

Schedule more time than you think you need to do the Between things.

Discernment

Just because you're good at something doesn't mean you should do it.

There are times when you have to dig really deep and put up with BS to get stuff done and get paid. I've been through a lot of those times personally. Unless you've been very lucky, you've been through those sorts of jobs, too. Those are stressful times, but they aren't exactly unexpected. Almost everyone has a story about a terrible job and it's usually one of their first jobs.

Those first jobs sometimes require you to put up things you will learn you won't tolerate later. You'll clean grease traps. You'll do the jobs that long-term employees have risen above. I hope you aren't stuck in a job where every day feels like the worst day of those first jobs. If so, do what you can to find other work and make new opportunities. Work on your resume, job skills and interviewing skills.

It may help you to keep in mind that sometimes losing a job or not getting a job is the best thing that could happen. One of my worst interview experiences was applying for a job I thought I needed. The interviewer was imperious and walked a line between cranky and rude. Unfortunately, he offered me the job.

As I was left to consider his offer I noticed another job candidate who had been waiting in the reception area walking to his car. He looked upset. After interviewing me, the guy who was to be my new boss had not had the courtesy to give the next candidate a chance at an interview. It was the middle of the workday. We both sacrificed time to attend the interview. That did not bode well for the future. I should have shut it down then but I was still trying to convince myself I needed the job at any cost.

In the second interview, it became obvious that I could not get along with this man. He rescinded the job offer before I got a chance to turn him down. Thank goodness. I would've been miserable there. As it turned out, a better job opportunity soon appeared.

Not every job will be the job of our dreams. However, watch out for warning signs so you know what you're getting into. Decide if the pain will be worth the gain. How does the boss treat his or her staff? When an interviewer says, "We've never been able to find anyone who can fulfill this position adequately," it's a bad sign. "Never," suggests they won't and can't be pleased.

Job interviews are stressful, mostly because of the power differential between the interviewer and the interviewee. There is an easy way to level up. Research your prospective employer. Come with your own set of questions. Be clear that you have value and much to offer. You are worthy of respect and the moment you stand for disrespect you have set a tone that can be very difficult to change. To bring the stress down, set your boundaries and your expectations. Evaluate your potential employer as they are evaluating you.

I'm under no delusion that this is possible for everyone at all times. However, get to that place as quickly as you can manage. Reset your attitude to convey that they need you — your talent and your value — as much as you need them. You may not be as valuable as all that to the company when you begin. However, by expanding your responsibilities and demonstrating growing capacity, you can soon become valuable.

**Do the walking away
thing when necessary.**

The Alphabet of Stress

For any stressful situation, you only have so many choices of how to deal with it. For years people talking about stress management would quote the 3 As strategy: Alter, Avoid, Accept.

Those are your options when you react to any stressor proactively: alter it, avoid it, accept it.

Go ahead.
Name any of your stressors.

1. Can you alter the situation to diminish your stress?

2. Can you avoid the situation to diminish your stress?

3. Can you accept the situation without trying to change it?

Good and useful questions, right? I notice the Mayo Clinic has added a fourth A: Adapt. That sounds to me a lot like more icing on a cake that's already pretty tall. Here's how I simplify the idea:

I deal with stresses using the 2 Es: Engage or Escape.

I can either avoid the problem (i.e. escape) or I can deal with it proactively (i.e. engage). Dealing with it might not mean fixing the problem. Not all problems can be fixed. The point of this chapter is to think of stressors categorically.

Ask yourself. Is your stressor something that is beyond your control? If so, don't worry about it. That's one way to escape it.

Is yours a stressor you can legitimately avoid without negative consequence? Escape.

Is this a stressor you can meet head on in some way? Engage.

The advantage of all these categories of thought is that they allow you to become objective. Evaluate courses of action in light of the amount of power you possess to meet those challenges. Your responsibility does not extend beyond your ability to respond.

Do the appropriate thing based on your ability to respond.

Do This Moment

I meditated for years, first as part of my martial arts training and later on my own. I went away from it but lately I've come back to it. If you're not a fan of meditation, I've got a trick that will make it much more palatable to you. But first, let's find the why, as in, why meditate?

Enthusiastic meditators often look much younger than their chronological age, so there's that. Regular practice reduces stress and brings an oasis of quiet in an unquiet world.

You don't have to be in a silent environment to meditate, of course. However, I do suggest you seek out quiet places when possible. Think about the noise pollution you are subjected to every day, for instance. Your car beeps just so you can unlock it with a remote. We are surrounded by disquiet: traffic, machinery, the blare of televisions, radios and whatever is on your headphones. Chronic elevated sound levels are associated with several health problems. Taking a few moments out of your day for quiet time is a healthier choice.

Mindfulness

Mindfulness is often considered its own sort of meditation. For my purposes here, I'm going to make a distinction between the two so you can apply both strategies when you are "officially" meditating and when you are just going about your normal day.

I think of mindfulness as the entry level of meditation. It will decrease your stress because you'll make fewer mistakes. If you pay attention to what you're doing the first time, you'll know if you locked your vehicle or left the dome light on. When you pay attention, you know where you parked the car when you come out of the mall an hour later. You can see where I'm going with this. Mindfulness is merely the singleminded attention to what you are doing. It's the opposite of multitasking.

Consider a walk down the street. If you pay attention, even a mundane scene can be a richer experience. I walk a lot. I look for differences and changes as I walk. Is the creek's water level higher or lower? Do I recognize anyone? How's the sunset tonight? A lot of people will tell you that if you aren't walking barefoot in the grass and appreciating nature every second, you aren't getting the most out of your day. I love walking in the city because so much changes and there are new things to see all the time.

Paying attention requires you to quiet the mind and be more receptive to what you see, hear, feel, touch and taste. If you're not sold on meditation, mindfulness is a good start and you'll reap many of the benefits. When you slow down and eat mindfully, for instance, you will enjoy your food more. You'll take the time to notice and savor the flavors.

Mindfulness, like meditation, cuts the stress because you are paying attention to the present moment. Stressed out people often complain of busy minds. They dwell on the regrets of the past and entertain anxiety about the future.

Monitor the stream of your thoughts. Regrets and anxieties tend to run in loops. Your mind may be occupied but it's busy with the same thoughts over and over. When you sense you're stuck in this unproductive loop, break the pattern by paying attention to what you can control in the present moment.

Do the mindful things.

Mindfulness and Meditation

I saw the great sci-fi writer Kurt Vonnegut give a speech on meditation. He explored the topic but, in his own inimitable way, he argued that the best meditation was to be found in reading a book. "In meditation," he said, "if you clear your mind and a blue scarf floats by, that's a major event." Fiction, he argued, allowed you to transport yourself elsewhere, be in two places at once and, at the height of the experience, be in other worlds.

As a calming exercise that sets time aside for you, I can't disagree with using reading as a meditative exercise. (I also write fiction and idolize Kurt Vonnegut. Of course, I'd feel that way.)

Let's talk more about formal meditation. Here are a few things you need to know:

1. To meditate, you do not have to be a vegan who meditates on a yoga mat in the full lotus position in a bamboo forest. A lot of us can't get into the full lotus position, so you'll probably be glad you can let that go. Many meditators simply sit toward the front edge of the seat of a chair with their back straight so they stay awake.

People who don't get enough quality sleep sometimes fall asleep during meditation. That's nice, but it's not the point of meditation. (If you can't stop yourself from falling asleep, read this chapter on Sleep Hygiene. You probably need it.)

2. Meditation is about focusing your mind.

I remember meditating in a public place. A girl I knew came up to me and said quite loudly, "You can hear me! You're not meditating! You're just sitting there with your eyes closed!" Sigh. I explained to her that, yes, I could indeed hear her. I was meditating. Meditation does not make you deaf.

3. Meditation is a practice for you. It is not necessarily a religious practice at all.

4. Meditation quiets the mind by giving it something specific to do. You can pay attention to the world around you and raise your

awareness externally. This is more on the mindfulness end of the meditation spectrum. You can pay attention to one thing, like your breath, to the exclusion of everything else.

Don't get frustrated. Your mind will interrupt your focus. "I'm hungry," "I'm tired," "I wonder what I'll do next," "I wish I'd punched that guy in sixth grade," etc.,... Gently bring your mind back to what your focus is, whether it's your breath, a repeated word or a sunset. It's okay that your mind interrupts you. Over time, your uninterrupted meditation time will lengthen.

5. There are moving meditations, too. I did Tai Chi for years. It was a set of 108 movements that were complicated enough that, while you were doing them, you didn't think of anything else. A friend who went scuba diving in winter reported a similar experience. Beneath the ice, he never thought about all the telephone calls he had to return. Down deep and focused, the world went away. He became so singleminded — immersed in the experience, if you will — nothing else existed during his dives.

6. Early on, I found myself frustrated with my meditation practice. I had a lot of rage and needed to contain it, but I also had a very active monkey mind to train.

Imagine your mind is a radio and your brain just spins that dial all day long searching for new stations but never staying on one channel very long. That's the monkey mind. Meditation helps to slow things down and ease up on all that stressful and unrelenting urgency we're constantly pelting ourselves with. Become still to quell all those errant thoughts but don't be impatient. Just keep doing it.

Start with short, concentrated bursts. The length of a single breath that you pay attention to can be a meditation. The length of a Tai Chi set can be twenty minutes. Start with a single breath. Then try one minute of meditation. Expand your time to five, ten or twenty minutes if you can.

7. Almost getting it. Meditation is a slippery thing. At first you'll get it in little bits, a little like going into the spaces between words in this sentence. As your concentration grows, you will quiet your mind enough that the space between words — the quiet times of the mind — get bigger. That's meditation.

You will slip into that quiet state and your monkey mind will shout, "Hey! I've got it! My mind is quiet." At least it was quiet until my brain shouted, "Hey! I've got it!" That's okay. Return to your focus.

8. Focusing on a mantra is effective for me. You simply repeat a word in your mind and bring your attention to that single focus. You can meditate on love or peace or use a nonsense word, like quan (a la the movie *Jerry McGuire*). I like monosyllabic mantras personally, although the word "mantra" will do fine, too. You'll be repeating it over and over in your mind so I think it's easier to keep your word short.

Some people use quite complex sentences in foreign languages that they don't necessarily fully understand. That's okay. It's just a device, a means to an end. The mantra is not the end in itself and there is nothing particularly mystical about it.

A long time ago a pair of meditators — a husband and wife — found a guru to teach them meditation. In separate ceremonies, one on one with the guru, he gave the husband and wife their very own super secret and special mantras to enrich their meditation practices. They weren't supposed to tell each other their mantras. Since they were married, they figured it was okay to whisper their secret to each other. You're probably already ahead of me in this story. The mantra was, of course, the same word.

The couple sued the guru. I don't know how it turned out, but I think they missed the point of bringing more peace to their minds.

9. Meditation can be boring. The best book on meditation I've ever read was *Full Catastrophe Living* by Jon Kabat-Zinn. His answer to the complaint that meditation was boring was, "So what?" A lot of things we should do for our health are boring. Brushing and flossing your teeth is boring but you probably make time for that (I hope).

What might sound like a somewhat callous response was actually quite freeing to me. I had a romantic notion of meditation at first. I thought it should be easier and somehow more magical than it turned out to be.

Now, I look at clearing my mind with the same attitude as I see any other exercise. I might not enjoy it but it is good for me and, as exercises go, it's not hard. Hold a plank position for five minutes. That's hard.

10. Make time for this. Meditation's benefits seem to outweigh the costs. You won't be able to perfect telepathy and it won't cure all that ails you. However, talk to a lot of productivity gurus, from pro biohacker Tim Ferriss to 5 AM morning guy Jeff Sanders, and you'll find a lot of successful people make time for meditation.

You might think rich people with empires to mind would have better things to do besides sitting crosslegged in their underwear first thing each morning. However, clearing your mind to come to a quiet focus sets a tone for the day. It brings all that noise down to a single signal.

Do the meditative thing.

My Meditation Hack

When I massage, I don't do anything else. The experience is richer for me and for the client on the table. My work is a meditation.

When I write, I am of a single focus. Whether I'm on the control deck of an airship in a world dominated by robots or under attack by zombies, as I write, I see it all. I am there. When I'm writing, I write and do nothing else. I stay in the meditative flow of creation. Writing (and reading) is a meditation.

When I set aside time to meditate, I don't ask more of myself than the span of a few deep abdominal breaths. I feel the benefits of slowing down and giving my nervous system the cue to settle down. It doesn't have to take a heavy time commitment, but I do it several times throughout the day.

Remember the feeling of relaxing into a quiet mind that is focused and you will return to that state.

Some meditators bring their thumb and forefingers together as a cue to return to that meditative state. They're conditioning themselves to slip into meditation using that simple physical cue. Try it and see if it works for you. When you come back to that focus several times a day, you don't have to reach far to get to that quiet space. The option is always waiting. Remember the feeling of that singleminded state of consciousness and, *whoosh*, you're back in it.

Meditation is not just for early mornings before tea in your dojo. It's there, all the time, waiting for you to turn off the monkey mind (or at least turn down the volume on the monkey mind).

Pay attention and return to the gaps between all those hurried, frenzied, blaring channels you call a day in your life.

Everything is not urgent.
You are not alone.
You can do this.

Do the things that will help get you where you wanted to be when you chose this book.

Visualization

Some clients rush in for their relaxation sessions with me. They get their hour of relaxation massage. Then they rush out. I feel like I've touched those clients but I haven't necessarily reached them.

I do not practice psychotherapy. I do sometimes close a relaxation massage with a visualization. This helps clients retain the benefits of treatment longer and allows them to reinforce the effect of treatment after they leave my treatment room. With the right visualization, you can connect to and remember the effects of treatment more deeply. With or without massage, I suggest you try visualization.

This tool can be very effective because the brain frequently does not distinguish between the real and unreal. (That's why dreams seem so real. It's why novels can transport you to other worlds. It's why you cry in movies.)

Visualizations are most helpful for mild to moderate pain and mild to moderate stress. If, during the course of this visualization, you become too uncomfortable to continue, open your eyes, get up and move around and expend your nervous energy in a healthy way. If you require a higher level of intervention, consult a health care professional. If you are comfortable with visualization as a stress and pain management tool, continue.

Lie on your back in a quiet room, door closed, cell phone off, no interruptions. Put a pillow beneath your knees and use a blanket if that makes you more comfy. The aim of this visualization is to deepen the relaxation experience and, with practice, this could become a useful tool to manage stress and low-grade pain.

Allow your eyes to close and your jaw to soften. You have nowhere else to be right now. Nothing else to do. With your hands at your sides, squeeze them into fists as tightly as is comfortable, just long enough to feel the tension build. Now relax your hands and feel the muscle tension drain away.

Take a long deep breath and then let it out slowly.

Bring your attention to your feet. Tighten the muscles of your feet and hold that squeeze just long enough to feel the full contraction of the muscles in the arches. Now relax those muscles. Note the difference between what you feel in your feet now compared to what you felt a moment ago.

Become aware of what tension may be left in the muscles of your feet. Without contracting a muscle, imagine that your feet are heavy, warm and relaxed. Now heavier, warmer and more relaxed.

Are your ankles tight or loose? As soon as you become aware of tension in your ankles, begin to let that tension drain away, too. Imagine the muscles lengthening and softening, releasing the tension in your feet wherever you find it, heavier, warmer and more relaxed.

When you feel the relaxation in your feet is complete, bring your attention up into your calves. Repeat the visualization *without* contracting a muscle. Release the tension wherever you find it by imagining the muscles in your calves are longer, softer and more relaxed...heavier, warmer and even more relaxed.

When you sense that process is complete, move on to your thighs and buttocks. Feel any tension there? Allow any tension you find there to drain away. As soon as you focus your attention on short and tight muscles, consciously let go of any tension you don't need.

Soft tissue should be soft. As you breathe slowly, deeply and abdominally, allow that feeling of lengthening and softening to spread up into your low back. Again, release tension wherever you find it. Your back is warmer, softer and more relaxed with each deep abdominal breath. Allow the bed to fully support you. Let your back sink into its support.

Bring your attention to the space between your body and the bed. As your body becomes heavier, warmer and more relaxed, imagine that you are closing that space between your body and the bed. Allow the bed to fully support you as you relax down into it.

If you find your mind wanders, that's fine. Breathe a little deeper and imagine your breath going into the area of tension. This will keep you present and engaged in the visualization.

Bring your attention to the space between your shoulders. Allow the warmth of relaxation to spread across your shoulder blades, heavier, softer and more relaxed. Allow your awareness of tension to do the work, bringing softness and length to each muscle.

Now try softening the muscles of your jaw. Let your teeth come slightly apart and wiggle your jaw back and forth a little if that feels comfortable for you. Allow the tension around your mouth to ease. As warm and relaxed as your body is, imagine your forehead is cool, released from tension and relaxed. Let go of the tension around your eyes.

Note the happy difference between tension and release, needless contraction and relaxation.

Allow your neck muscles to release and relax, lengthen and soften. You may imagine that your head weighs 1000 pounds. Now imagine that your head weighs 1100 pounds... 1200 pounds... 13... 1400 pounds. There is no need for your neck to carry that weight. Let the bed fully support the weight of your head as the muscles of your neck yield to gravity, release the tension, relax the muscle, soften the tissue, ease the needless strain.

Warm, calm and relaxed, scan your body for any residual areas of tension. If you feel you are making an effort, now is the time to release any sense of urgency. Don't try to make relaxation occur. Relaxation is muscle *not* contracting. Allow relaxation to happen.

Take another slow, deep abdominal breath. Let it out slowly.

Scan your body and note the difference in your body's tension from a few minutes ago.

Remember this feeling of conscious relaxation. With practice, you will be able to enter this relaxed state more quickly and naturally.

Remember this feeling so you can come back to it at anytime. Relaxation is not just for short and special moments of time. Relaxation is accessible and can be practiced on a regular basis. Escape from needless tension is not limited to massage treatment rooms and yoga mats.

Remember this feeling and you can come back to it at anytime: when you are stressed, when you're in pain, when you want to go to sleep, remember this relaxed feeling so you can more easily repeat it. This feeling is yours to keep now.

As you make this visualization a regular practice, consistency will bring you deeper into the experience. You can ease your tension with attention.

Do the visualization thing.*

*I know you can't read all this and do it at the same time. I will put up this chapter as my first episode of the all-new All That Chazz Stress Relief podcast starting in the second week of January 2017. Go to AllThatChazz.com for the podcasts and updates.

Hypnagogic State

When you are looking for answers to questions and solutions to problems, a magic eight ball is not your best choice. However, I do have a little trick that has proven very valuable. As a frequent podcast guest, I speak to writers about creativity and solving plot problems. What I am about to impart to you is something that I have found very useful for all kinds of problems that require lateral thinking or a fresh take.

I've been using this tool for so long that I have forgotten where I first picked it up. It is called the hypnagogic state. When I get stuck on a life problem, I have often found that is a good time to have a rest and let the answer come on its own. You've already had an inkling of this experience when you try to remember a particular word. Sometimes the answer really feels like it's on the tip of your tongue but the longer and harder you try to think of the word, the more it eludes you. When you consciously ignore the question and put your mind to something else, in time, the word you searched for so desperately comes to mind. The hypnagogic state feels a little like that to me in practice.

Hypnagogia refers generally to the transition states from wakefulness to sleep and from sleep to wakefulness. I use this technique almost every night on some vexing problem or other. As you go to sleep, you might think of the first stage as a hypnotic suggestion. I ask myself a question as I fall asleep, confident that the answer will arrive as I awake.

When morning comes, in that special time between sleeping, dreaming and waking, my thoughts will be more lucid than during a normal consciousness. For perhaps 20 to 30 seconds a day, I'm a genius. My thoughts are clear and I can see through problems and receive answers that would not come if I worked at arriving at it using normal consciousness.

Hypnagogia is an incredibly creative state and it has a long history. The phenomenon was even mentioned by Aristotle. Such visionaries as Tesla, Beethoven and Salvador Dali have claimed its use in their work. Charles Dickens mentions it in *Oliver Twist*.

August Kekulé famously discovered the ring structure of benzene while half-asleep.

While working on my first crime thriller, my habit was to write a chapter a day. I didn't work from an outline. I had no idea how I would continue the story the next day. This wasn't as momentous as discovering the structure of benzene but it was surprisingly challenging. In my novels, Jesus Diaz is an assassin with a particular talent for getting into trouble. Each night, I left Jesus in a dangerous place, seemingly with no way out. Each morning, the next plot point arrived right on time.

I have found that to extend the hypnagogic state it is helpful to get to bed early or at least do not wake up to an alarm. An alarm clock will bring you out of sleep too quickly with little time to divine your semi-conscious genius.

Ask yourself the question each night as you fall asleep. Each morning, languish in bed an extra few moments, pause and, as you swim up to consciousness, let the answers come.

Do the hypnagogic thing.

SECTION II

TIME MANAGEMENT

Ready to Do The Thing?

Let's do the thing!
Let's do all the things!*

*Unless, of course, that's overwhelming. In which case, do *a* thing.

The Obstacles at Your Feet

Comedian Duncan Trussell gave some advice on his podcast (*The Duncan Trussell Family Hour*) which really resonated with me. He suggested that if your life is off the rails, start getting your life together by cleaning your house. Maybe this sounds goofy to you at first but give this idea a chance. How much time do you waste searching for misplaced things? Those envelopes, the stamps and the stapler are not technically lost, I know. They're around your desk somewhere, but where?

How many times have you created stress by misplacing your keys, glasses or phone? Sure, everyone wants to blame Mort in accounting, but Mort didn't leave your phone on the window ledge by the toilet. You did. Mort didn't hide your keys in the living room couch. You know you should have hung those keys on the hook by the door. Stop blaming Mort for everything.

If you drop a grape by your desk and it takes you a few minutes to find it, it's definitely time to clean up around your desk. (Yes, that happened to me.)

There's something deeper going on in your mind when you finally get around to cleaning up your house and office. You find things you forgot you had. You find duplicates of items. You don't have to buy new pens. You already have plenty of pens. You'll discover correspondence you should have dealt with already. You'll find clothes you haven't worn in a long time. If they still fit, wear them and you've saved a trip to the store and money, too.

When you discover all the junk you don't need, get rid of it. If you need the dough, have a yard sale if you must. (I hate yard sales and the shoppers looking to haggle me down to a nickel.) Take the stuff you don't need to Goodwill and enjoy all the new space in your house. Most people don't need to add another room to their house. They just need to better use the space they already have. People who live in houseboats and mobile homes all know, most people surround themselves with way too much stuff they don't need.

Once the junk goes out the door, don't let it back in.

That which doesn't sell in that yard sale can still be reused. Donate old books to libraries. Take clothes to consignment stores but, again, if it doesn't sell, it doesn't come back in your house. It's getting in the way. It's cluttering your life. Hoarders are not productive people. They are sad people. Don't be one. (Full disclosure: I have a book collection problem. I'm working on it. Hey, I never said I was perfect.)

Clean house and clear your mind. In an uncluttered space, the productive mind is unfettered and can finally get down to being productive. You'll know where the paperclips are. You won't waste time searching through piles of paper for that one piece of information you need.

Do the clear thing.

Decluttering doesn't stop with folding your socks. On the next page, let's go deeper.

Look for Something You Don't Have To Do

I'm an entrepreneur. I run four businesses. I have to manage my time carefully to stay on top of all I have to do. I'm vigilant about things that are a waste of time. I think you should be, too. Here are some examples I hope you'll find useful.

A writer friend was interviewing me on a podcast recently. He asked how I formulated my business plans.

"I don't."

This is, of course, heresy. There are plenty of business books and so-called experts pushing their agenda: make a business plan or you'll fail. It's supposed to be a useful exercise. However, I'm not looking to borrow money from a bank and I'm not sucking up to a venture capitalist. I'm an independent contractor, a freelancer, a solo entrepreneur. I have a couple of business partners with whom I almost always agree. In short, I don't need a business plan. Unless you're applying for a loan, managing a large enterprise or building a turnkey operation you plan to franchise, you probably don't need a business plan, either.

Naturally, I got some resistance to this idea. However, I haven't had a single boss since 1992. For many serial entrepreneurs, business plans are forgotten things that, once created, are never read twice. One day, when you find that business plan you slaved over at the back of a drawer, you're in for a good laugh.

Here's another secret: Business plans for new companies are bullshit. Those projections are based on optimism and fairy dust. Without experience and a track record, no business owner will know that July and February will be their slowest months. They won't know which marketing plans will work and what won't. For new ventures, a business plan is usually a hope and a dream disconnected from the rigors of reality. I created a business plan for my first business (to get seed money). I got the seed money and never looked at the business plan again. Or any other business plan. For me, it was a useless exercise.

Do you really need a business plan? Maybe. Maybe not. Only you can evaluate your individual needs. However, what you do need is a *schedule*.

Do the time management thing.

If you can do without a business plan, do without it. However, you do need commitments and schedules. Turn the page for more on that.

When a Little is Still Too Much...

Years ago, I was on vacation in British Columbia when I ran across an unusual book. It was about stress management but it was specifically written for clergy. I'm not religious now but I was in those days. I thought a friend of mine, the pastor of a large church, needed the help. I delivered the book to him in his office after the next Sunday service.

When I walked in, the Rev's usual sunny demeanor was muted. He'd had colon cancer once. He'd had it treated and all was well for a while. I'll never forget the look in his eyes when he told me that day, "The cancer is back."

We talked about several things in the minutes that followed. He spoke of how he'd have to step back from his busy ministry to pursue further treatment. He worried about the course of treatment ahead. He worried that the treatment might fail. He was also very concerned for the fate of his family and the church he had built. The demands of a large and growing congregation were many. How could he step back and what would life look like then? Even without the cancer diagnosis, the work had taken a toll on him. Everyone loved him. Sometimes, too much was asked of him because everyone wanted to spend time with the Rev.

I pledged to be part of his support team, of course. "You're here for everyone else, Rev. I'm here for you."*

Suddenly, my gift was even more timely. I'd read the stress management book and gave him a few of the highlights as I handed it over. "The author said something interesting I think you'll relate to. For clergy, each member of their church is a mouse and you're the cheese. Each mouse just wants one bite."

At that moment, someone pounded on his office door impatiently. Our meeting had apparently gone on too long for someone's taste. The pastor looked to the door and smiled, "It's the mice! *It's the mice!*"

We'd begun with very bad news. Still, we broke into laughter at the end.

Do the jokey thing.

*Hint: Thoughts and prayers are nice. What's better is giving patients rides to and from doctor appointments, being ready to help however they need help and sending over a casserole etc.,...)

When People Ask Too Much

When people ask for too much, say no. Don't feel you have to explain yourself when you say no. "I have other plans," "that doesn't fit into my schedule," "I can't make it," whatever, if you feel you must. Polite people don't demand justifications for how you spend your time. (Hang out with polite people.)

Only you can tell when what is asked is too much. Do not let others determine how much help you can stand to give them.

Do the assertive thing.

How Do I Say No When So Many Depend On Me?

I'm not telling you to say no to everything. In fact, I'm not telling you to do anything at all. It's up to you to do what you will with the information in this book. I will ask you to evaluate the consequences of your response to the demands of others:

Helping others feels good, doesn't it? Sure it does!

Until it doesn't. When you give all the time, you burn out. Then you will be less helpful. This is not just a matter of time management. It is a matter of energy management. Both resources are finite, so dole them out accordingly.

Helping out feels nice and is also a gift to the person doing the helping.

I get a lot of satisfaction in my job. I help people and, when I tell them something they've never heard before, it makes me feel smart and useful. We help others because we're people pleasers who want to be liked. We want to feel valued. Be careful that you don't work too hard for people who don't value you.

Years ago, I had a client who had a lot of stress and physical concerns. For every remedial exercise and tip I proposed, she had an excuse as to why it was impossible for her to help herself. Still, she sat in my office asking questions and rejecting my answers. Finally, I said, "How about deep abdominal breathing? Surely you've got time for that."

"I work in government," she said. "They don't give us time for deep breathing."

Message received. I've had the same conversation with my kids. They'll tell me there's no food in the house. I'll make thirteen meal recommendations based on what I can find in the kitchen cupboards, the freezer and the fridge. To which they reply, "No, no, no. Let's order pizza."

The lady who rejected a deep breath as too demanding of her time didn't want help. She didn't want solutions. She wanted a sympathetic ear. I gave her a sympathetic hearing but I didn't waste any more breath on answers she wasn't interested in trying out.

Help others.

Empower them to help themselves.

Do not enable them.

**If you're more invested in a positive outcome than the person you are helping,
you aren't helping them.
Worse, they may be hurting you.**

Do the things that really help.

The Replacements

We hear a lot about all the things we should not do. For instance, the ten commandments are very focused on what we should not do. Funny how humans think. As soon as something is forbidden, it's often more alluring. However, if you focus on all the things you should do, you won't have much time to think about the things you shouldn't.

When I'm taking the time to cut up fruits and vegetables and broiling my chicken breasts for the week, I'm avoiding a lot of last-minute decisions that would lead me to fast food drive-throughs. This principle applies to thoughts as much as it does to food prep. Replacement thinking substitutes positive self-talk for negative self-talk.

You can observe this mind trick most clearly with children. Kids fall down and skin their knees a lot. They cry easily. When I became a father, I soon found out that I could joke my kids out of minor injuries. They'd fall down and cry and I'd do something silly to make them laugh. You can make a child laugh, kiss the boo boo better and make the pain go away while the child still has undried tears on his or her cheeks.

Your thoughts lead you to whatever state you're in.

Think negative thoughts and you'll soon find yourself in a negative state. Watch news channels devoted to making you fearful and you'll be fearful. Dwell on anger and you'll be angry. It's not that complicated, so change it. Replace the negative with the positive and take positive action. (This book is full of positive actions you can take so take a sample from the idea buffet and try it.)

Don't just think positive. Do the positive thing, too.

Productive at What?

A lot of the undone things are left undone for a reason. Sometimes those reasons are valid. Maybe you shouldn't do them.

Do the discerning thing.

Busy or Productive?

There's a huge difference between acting busy and being productive. For instance, do you know someone who is very proud that they are first to arrive in the company parking lot each morning and last to leave each night? They seem to be at work constantly But are they productive and efficient? Often, these folks don't take recovery time. Though their bodies are at the office, their pace and production is slow. Their work expands to fill all that extra time they impose on themselves. They must be exhausted. They hardly go home!

What counts is getting things done, not the amount of time spent to get things done.

You must allow enough time for any given task. Be careful not to allow too much time. I wrote the first draft to one of my crime thrillers in eighteen days. That speed is my personal best, but the experience also reset my expectations for how long it should take me to write any book. For this book, for instance, most of the research was already complete before I began to write. My first professional training was as a journalist. Since my training was to meet short deadlines, I work to that expectation. I've published five books in a year but I have several friends who write faster than that.

First Rule of Productivity

Busyness is not business. Your capacity to produce is largely about perception.

When I worked in the traditional publishing industry, the work pace was glacial. Even if authors wrote a book quickly, publishers could take years to get their books into bookstores. This slow progress was, by the accounts of all experts of the time, necessary. Part of the problem was institutional. Not enough resources were devoted to complete the necessary tasks and they worked with small budgets and a minuscule number of staff.

This was true of most of the industry. However, my first jobs in publishing were at Harlequin. A huge romance publisher, the company's system was set for high productivity. They published 80 titles a month and they had the staff and capacity to hit that target every month. Many of their competitors would take a year, two, or even more to hit that level of productivity.

Second Rule of Productivity

Time spent surfing Facebook, cruising YouTube and watching Netflix doesn't count toward your work hours.

There are still writers who write slowly and I do not denigrate them. Everyone should write at the pace they can manage that produces their best work. However, procrastination is not work. When a writer says, "It took me three years to write my book," they're including all the time they spent eating, sleeping and doing other things. How many hours a week did they really devote to writing? If that writer recorded their *actual* writing time it would be far less than three years.

Third Rule of Productivity: That which is not measured is not changed.

I know a CEO who went to work very early in the morning. Through experience, he learned that he got most of his work done before 8:30 a.m. After that, a parade of interruptions began. A work study that measured productive time for business owners found that CEOs had an average of seven minutes of work between interruptions.

My friend had an elegant solution to this problem. He came in early and left early. He worked from home later in the day. Most important, he trained his staff well. They became qualified and empowered to work autonomously. He accomplished this so well that, when he did appear in the office, he felt a tad irrelevant.

This was very good for the staff, as well. When people are trusted to act on their own to solve more problems, those problems are solved faster. Responsibility conveys value. People who feel like they have some control over their work environments are happier people. (See the chapter titled What's Your Button? for why that is.)

Do the productive things.

Solutions to the Big To-do.

Remember I mentioned the guy who thought the one answer to dealing with stress is to get everything done? If you have a really short list of things to do and you can actually strike tasks off in a short time, that's great. There's a wonderful feeling of accomplishment in clearing off assigned tasks. However, this is a flawed strategy because, in the real world, the to do list never ends. Let's get real about to do lists.

Too many tasks fail to fall into a handy time slot where you can begin and complete a task at once. Unless your to do list includes very small tasks like making your bed, you won't have the fun of striking off many items on your list.

Don't include normal routine tasks on your to do list. Making your bed, brushing your teeth, showering, shaving etc.,... doesn't need to be on your to do list because it is routine. The person who commits to roll out of bed and pump out fifty pushups doesn't need to have a list as a reminder. It's just the thing to do every day.

To do lists are time consuming in their creation and should have a definite purpose other than making the list. The goal of a to do list is to make one you will use to get stuff done. The goal is not to create a long list of unaccomplished tasks that make you feel guilty. Do not add to your workload in the name of efficiency.

Larger tasks usually have to be broken up into bite-sized pieces. So what's the solution to the problem of the long to do list?

I don't have one solution. I have several, but the list won't be so long that it's overwhelming.

Do the routine things without making a list.

Up next, quick suggestions will outline how to manage your time and energy to manage your stress and increase your power.

Use the Power of the Swoop

What's the Swoop? It's picking up the laundry on your way downstairs. It's putting dirty dishes straight in the dishwasher instead of in the sink or on the counter. The Swoop isn't a list. It's being aware of the small opportunities to do something quick without it becoming a chore. The Swoop is about efficiency, cleaning as you go, rather than allowing tasks to pile up.

These small efficiencies take less time. Even better, it's time expended that you won't even notice. No to do list required.

I swooped this idea from an old roommate who was neater than me.
Do the tidy thing.

Delegate

Are you taking on too much responsibility?

Are you the sort who does his or her tasks and everyone else's work, too? For some, the charge they get from acting this way is about control. There is drama in bulling your way in and throwing your weight around with a false sense of urgency. There's more stress for you and everyone else, too. (And you're here for less stress, right?)

Remember, the captain of the ship does not go down to the engine room. That is the engineer's domain. Too many stressed out captains are swabbing the decks instead of doing their own job and steering clear of the icebergs ahead.*

Do not micromanage others.

Micromanagers crowd everyone. If you stick your nose in everywhere, others will resent you for taking away their power. Trust people more so you have time to focus on what you are best at. Let them feel they're good at something, too.

Workplaces that disempower employees have a high turnover rate. If you are constantly dissatisfied with employee performance or you have to find new staff frequently, something's wrong. It might be you.

Do the self-aware thing.

*If you are the staffer who is being micromanaged, give this book as a gift to your oppressor. Maybe they will recognize themselves, take the hint and manage their stress better (so their stress doesn't become yours.)

See also, the chapter titled Reactivity.

Like Me, Love Me, Hurt Me

Maybe you do respect others and you aren't a micromanager. Perhaps you try to do everyone else's job because you are a people pleaser. That way madness lies.

If you have kids who can walk and carry things, they can get their own dishes back to the dishwasher and make their own beds. Catch them early enough and they'll actually be enthused about washing their own clothes. They can't claim helplessness at fifteen if they did it when they were seven. Many hands make light work and less stress.

At the office, beware of people who take advantage of their own helplessness. By that I mean that there is always someone who has never learned how to use the photocopier. Don't do it for them. Train them.

Every office has a mom or dad type who falls into doing tasks for others. In the short-term, it is often quicker to do those tasks for others. This is false efficiency. In the long-term, they're stealing time from you accomplishing your tasks. When work roles are better defined and those boundaries are adhered to, the workplace is more efficient.

Do the responsible thing.
Don't be responsible for everything.

Unleash Time

My wife and I have a housekeeper. I used to think that was a luxury. Why pay someone else to do what we could do ourselves for free? Isn't it an unnecessary expense? In our case, our housekeeper is absolutely necessary.

My wife and I have multiple jobs and our schedules are jigsaw puzzles that have to be tweaked so all the pieces fit together. While the housekeeper does her job, we use the freed time to write more books and get more stuff done that pays.

It makes financial sense but I call it marriage insurance. We don't have to worry about whose turn it is to clean the bathtub. Outsourcing unleashes time so we can focus elsewhere. I'm not suggesting that everyone should get a maid. I do want you to think about how you can apply this principle to your life and work.

To figure out your wiggle room, calculate how much you make per hour. Don't count your gross. What's your net income per hour? That's your number. If you can hire someone to do one of your chores while you use that time to make more money, consider doing so.

There is an important caveat, however.

More money doesn't necessarily mean less stress and this book *is* about stress management. Suppose you can hire a kid in your neighborhood to mow your lawn. For a few bucks, there's an opportunity for you to use the time more efficiently for work. CEOs don't mow their lawns and maybe you shouldn't, either.

But what if you enjoy mowing the lawn?

One of the keys to stress management is getting things done to receive that little boost of dopamine in your brain. Many of our tasks fail to punch up that happy neurotransmitter because there's no sense of finality to many tasks. There is no finish line at the end of the work day with fans cheering you on and waving flags. You have to take your perks where you find them.

I have allergies that only seem to be getting worse. I love to pay someone else to mow my lawn. However, what's right for me might not be right for you. If you love the smell of fresh cut grass, maybe you don't *want* to hire the neighbor's kid to mow your lawn. Maybe mowing the lawn is a point of pride. Maybe the chore is a rare chance to unwind, get some exercise and think of nothing much in particular. That peace of mind could be worth a few bucks and its cheaper than a meditation retreat in the Andes, right?

Maybe more CEOs should mow their lawns after all. Time is not merely money. Time is life. Time is not an unlimited resource. Spend wisely.

Do your thing.

To Don't

A to do list is only useful if it facilitates action. Chances are excellent your list is too long. Realistic goals lead to feelings of accomplishment, encourage action and gain momentum. Unrealistic lists make you feel like a failure. Then you'll probably stop making any list and take much less action.

I love my to don't list. It's all the stuff I don't waste time writing down that I can't realistically accomplish. A to do list is only useful if it is used. Keep it short and keep it real.

But how long should your to do list really be?

Here's your answer:

Dig out your crumpled Post-it note or wherever you keep your to do list. Have a hard look at the last several days. How much is crossed off that list?

If you've got ten items but you only cross off two each day, two items is ideal for you.

For the rest, you don't need a to do list. You need a calendar. Calendars are for long-term planning. No more getting overwhelmed with that long daily list of unaccomplished tasks. It will all get done, but not all in one day. Stop torturing yourself and adding to your stress.

To do lists are for daily tasks that you are likely to get done. The long-term plans on your calendar determine what items that will go on your to do list each day. Stay real. Writing down your long-term goals and organizing your calendar is a helpful exercise. Don't confuse all those many tasks with a to do list.

There are undoubtedly suggestions I'll give you in this book that won't be right for you. They'll be right for someone else. Don't worry about what you won't do. Do what you will do.

Do your thing well.

Stress Crusher

Use Google Calendar to set up reminders of tasks, meetings and deadlines. Allot enough time to accomplish your tasks and organize your days. Nothing will fall between the cracks and you'll experience much less stress. Do this much (this little?) and soon you could be busting stress with a To Done list.

Do the stress crushing thing and turn the page.

To Done

People make lists because they're worried they'll forget important tasks. Spreading out your tasks on a calendar and setting reasonable deadlines is much more in line with reality and how people actually work. When you aren't worried about losing a task in the mix, you have the power to choose the joy of a to done list.

People who manage their time well (and don't overwhelm themselves with long lists of daily tasks) may choose to get their dopamine hits in a different way. Instead of writing down what you must do each day, write what you *did*.

Lists can be intimidating, overwhelming and draining. A to done list is an energy building strategy. You build momentum by compiling a list of tasks *after* you've got each item done.

In your to don't list, you got realistic. You avoided listing stuff you wouldn't get done anyway. Your goal was to kill it and cross tasks off your to dos.

In your to done list, you have your calendar to track what needs to be done but you begin each day with a *blank* sheet. Only add to the list the things you actually accomplish. This can be an effective mind trick. It feels good to add to that list of things done, plus you have no leftover tasks to carry over to tomorrow!

Experiment
Which list strategy, building or killing, works best for you?
To do or to done?

Do more of what works for you.
Do the stress less thing.

Break Time Part I

Imagine you are driving a car without brakes. You push the accelerator to the floor and hold it there to go as fast as you can. How long before you crash or the engine blows up? Unfortunately, that's how some people try to live their lives.

Work without breaks is not the most productive work. The more fatigued you are, the more mistakes will be made. Airlines have recognized this fact and have instituted rules for pilots so they get more sleep than they used to.

Unfortunately, teaching hospitals are still behind the curve in this regard. Medical schools are still working on inertia from earlier days, forcing med students to endure long hours without sufficient rest. This bootcamp mentality — "I suffered through it so you have to!" — has resulted in errors in a work environment where errors are deadly.

Do the well rested thing.

Break Time Part II

To enhance your productivity, how much rest do you need?

I wish I could give you one simple number. However, your need for rest will vary depending on many variables. To name a few, how much sleep did you get last night? What is the task? Are we talking about sitting, standing or heavy labor for long periods? What time of day are you working and when are you most effective? Are you feeling energized or do you want to flip your desk over, stagger out into the sunshine and scream, "Freedom!" while tearing off your clothes? Do you nap and for how long?

You're going to have to experiment to divine your optimal break times. Do the most important and challenging work when you are most energized. People make impulsive and poor decisions when they are fatigued. Your tiredness is what makes all those late night info commercials more appealing. Fatigue can make you just as dangerous a driver as alcohol.

Get enough rest so you wake up refreshed.* Then do the thing.

*You'll find sleep hygiene suggestions, power nap tricks and a lifesaving tip about sleep apnea in the Energy Management section of this guide.

Break Time Part III

For a sense of the diversity of the problem of adequate rest, consider high school students. Adolescents require more sleep. Their bodies are growing and changing enormously. However, most schools function on a schedule that starts them off early each morning. Progressive schools will one day reevaluate why they do things the way they do. They will match the school schedule to students' biorhythms.

A note for students and their parents:

Get involved with your school and parent councils to begin the process of changing the educational system where it does not serve you. Some schools are reevaluating how much homework children have to do each night, for instance. Often, far too much homework is assigned to little purpose. Progress is being made slowly. Take heart. The system has changed elsewhere, so you can change it, too.*

From my research, several sources suggest there *are* optimal times for learning new tasks. Not all decision-making is equal. Not all tasks require the same level of attention. Your mileage will vary. For instance, if your eyes glaze over when someone is trying to teach you algebra, you'll need more frequent breaks and more sleep to absorb and retain the new information.

A good night's sleep is critical to assimilating learning into long-term memory. That's why last-minute panic cramming for exams is so counterproductive compared to a slow, steady study schedule. To absorb, retain and recall new data, you must sleep.

Do the biorhythmic thing.

*For more on this topic, I recommend you consider Finland's success in improving their school system. Michael Moore's documentary *Where to Invade Next?* has a very hopeful and thought-provoking segment on this topic.

The Consistency Trick

Many of us feel like we're in the rat race. The story of the tortoise and the hare may be more instructive.

We all know the story. The hare loses to the tortoise. I think the story gets it wrong, though. We're told the hare lost the race because, though he was fast, he was arrogant. He took a nap while the tortoise kept steadily plodding to the finish line. I think that if you take the fable of the tortoise and the hare seriously, the tortoise would win not just because he kept trying but because he *lives* far longer.

Try to do too much and you'll burn out. Juggling a lot of tasks is sexier, though, isn't it? There's drama (and big buckets of myth) around the rugged individualist who bends the world to his or her will. In theory, going solo seems strong and brave. We'd much rather be Tony Stark inventing the Iron Man suit alone over a harried, sleepless week or two. On screen, you won't see Robert Downey Jr. filing a patent or getting a license for a nuclear reactor in his basement. Fiction doesn't fit reality. Entrepreneurs need teams. Even the smallest business needs a support team. Successful people are deal makers and collaborators.

Most productivity comes from consistency. Do not trust energy spikes to get work done. Hurried work makes more errors. Fortunately, a little work done consistently builds up quickly. If I write 2,500 words a day every day, I have a draft for the average length of one of my books in a month. For me, that's a couple of hours a day. Suddenly, writing a book doesn't sound like such a huge time commitment, does it?

This principle is applicable to you in many ways. In my work as a massage therapist, I review stretches with clients. I encourage them to *enjoy* stretching. "Feel a pull, not a pain. A good stretch feels *good*!" Stretching a little each day is more effective in all its aspects. Better to stretch six days a week than to try to cram all your week's stretching into one Sunday afternoon.

Our minds and bodies respond to persuasion, not coercion. If you don't floss for a week, don't try to catch up on all the flossing you missed the morning of your next dental checkup. Those bloody gums are not fooling your dentist. Occasionally, a flurry of action at the end of a project will make the difference in getting it done, shipped or sold faster. However, it's all the consistent action long before that last minute that did the bulk of the work.

Do the tortoise thing and live longer.

An Hour a Day

If someone said you had to take an hour out of your day to do something, how much resistance would you feel? For most of us — stressed, obsessed, pressed and possibly depressed — an hour devoted to one more chore feels like too much of a demand. Our schedules are packed too tight.

As I was writing this book, I was diagnosed with an eye problem. I have dry eye disease. There is no cure but it can be managed. Among other things, the doctor told me I had to put heat on my eyes and rest for an hour a day. Fortunately, I could break it up into four fifteen-minute segments. Suddenly, an hour out of the day doesn't sound so bad, does it?

If you can't find four intervals of fifteen minutes, your day is overstuffed. Slow down.

Though my eye problem is an annoyance, I find those fifteen minute breaks in the dark are a needed break. A little quiet time, less stimulus and time to think (or not think) should be part of every day.

Do the restful thing before your doctor tells you it's a must.

How to Guard Your Time

The distractions of the internet can educate, entertain, build dreams or ruin all your hopes. Stay in charge of your time.

1. Work behind closed doors.

2. If the closed door doesn't work, educate others in what a closed door means so they know you're serious.

3. Get a do not disturb sign and use it.

4. Get a lock for your office door.

5. Get out of the house or office to work.

6. Don't answer the phone if you don't recognize the number.

7. Block telemarketers. Ban door-to-door salespeople.

8. Your new policy is that no interruption is small.

9. Unplug the phone.

10. Unplug the internet.

11. When people demand your time, schedule them.

12. Arrange your life or you'll be pushed and pulled in all directions.

13. When people come into your office, don't invite them to sit.

14. Look busy and people will disturb you less often.

15. Hold meetings at the end of the day when everyone is eager to go home instead of making the meeting a social occasion.

16. Have standing meetings so people don't get comfortable and settle in.

17. When problems are presented, ask for options and solutions from the person bringing up the problem.

18. Train, educate and empower others to solve problems.

Do the things that defend your time.

Sadly, there is no shortage of books that tell you to stick to your plans to achieve your goals. There are fewer books that tell you how. Let's dive into that next in *How to Stick*.

How to Stick

When you set out to accomplish a task, write it in your calendar. Without planning ahead, you're bound to fail.

To manage your stress and energy, prioritize your goal by getting it done when you are at your peak energy. Many people mean to exercise daily but they don't get around to it. I advise you to treat exercise like a medical appointment. If you don't make time for exercise, you'll end up having more medical appointments. Getting and staying healthy is easier and healthier than treating disease so there's that.

Don't just remind yourself of important tasks daily. Some tasks require you to keep your motivation going hourly or even more often. To succeed, keep your prime motivator top of mind.

The task, for instance, is:

Go to the gym.

The schedule is:

Go to the gym at 7 a.m. to get to work by 9 a.m.

Your motivator is:

I go to the gym at 7 a.m. to get to work by 9 a.m. because I'll feel so much better and healthier when I'm done.

Write down all your motivators and review them often. To memorize a song, you have to sing it often. It's the same with the things you do to get things done. In the same tune as this example, you might have one or several of the following motivators:

I go to the gym and eat well because my high school reunion is next year and I want to look good.

I want to be able to go kayaking and I have to train for that.

I want to enjoy my life with more energy.

I want a high quality of life as I age.

When I work out, I feel like the person I'm supposed to be.

Now find *your* motivators for important tasks.

Scare tactics don't last. Shame could drive you to seek comfort where you shouldn't. Shame can spur you to self-medicate with unhealthy foods or other substances. Keep your motivators positive and hopeful and remind yourself of your goals as often as it takes.

Do all the things that motivate you (without shame.)

Stress Management: The Deeper Dive

Everyone needs a support network. Lonely people need friends. Even introverts benefit from social interaction. We are programmed to be social. Even in prison, the worst thing the authorities can legally do to you is keep you in isolation, away from fellow inmates.

Stressed out and lonely? I can't save you. You can save yourself with a little help from your friends. If you don't have friends, that's the first stress factor you need to address. Just like you were taught in elementary school, be a friend to get a friend.

Do the friendly thing.

About Doing Hard Things

It's standard advice in stress management books to do the hard thing first. Eat a toad first thing in the morning and the rest of the day will look easier. I don't disagree. You don't need a lot of preamble and ritual around it, either. Just dive in and get the difficult tasks out of the way so they aren't hanging over you all day. That's a formula to drain your energy. (See the chapter on energy management for a caveat on this, though.)

But let's go deeper than the standard stress management advice.

In this book, using cues and time management, I generally try to make your stress management efforts easier, faster and less intimidating. However, easy doesn't motivate everyone. Recently, I read *Presto!* by Penn Jillette. The famous magician details how he lost roughly 100 pounds in a remarkably short time. It wasn't easy and that's one of the motivators that attracted Jillette to the program.

As a magician, he works hard to make his tricks look smooth and easy. However, he was a juggler first. If juggling looks easy, it's not impressive. He enjoys making things difficult. Eating nothing but potatoes for fifteen days was hard. (He then transitioned to eating a plant-based diet. Read *Presto!* for more details. There's a lot more to the story than eating potatoes and Jillette is an entertaining storyteller who is now much lighter than he used to be.)

Kennedy set a goal of going to the moon, "not because it's easy but because it is hard." That's attractive to some people. A hard regimen (well-planned and executed) is attractive *because* it's radical. For my own weight loss, I found Penn Jillette's story reassuring. He made me feel less anxious about going hungry and to welcome hunger pangs. Many of us in First World countries are constantly eluding any discomfort. When I changed my mindset to look on hunger pangs as a normal part of life, I felt less compelled to self-medicate with food.

All change is uncomfortable. Progress doesn't grow inside the dark confines of our tight comfort zones.

Do the uncomfortable thing.

Deciding

In the book *Body for Life*, author Bill Phillips suggests a powerful tool that guides what you allow yourself to eat. He talks about the question in terms of "authorized foods." You can eat this because it's on your authorized food list. You can't eat that because it's not on the authorized foods list. In other words, you've made a decision and you're sticking to it.

Half-measures can sabotage achievement.

If you tell yourself you can get away with eating half a bag of chips, will you actually stop at half a bag? Does anybody? Will you eat seven almonds for dessert or will the whole bag be gone by tomorrow?

In *Dead Again*, Robin Williams' character is a former psychologist. Kenneth Branagh is trying to quit smoking. Williams advises him, "Someone is either a smoker or a nonsmoker. There's no in-between. The trick is to find out which one you are, and be that."

Do the decisive thing.*

*Tailor your environment for success. If you don't have the chips in the house, you are less likely to act on impulse for that craving.

More on Staying Sticky

You may never be early for your colonoscopy but you'll never be late for it, either. We take medical appointments seriously. A meeting with a doctor excuses us from work. We will wait in a waiting room a long time because, damn it, those checkups and test results are important!

Newsflash:
You're important all the time. People love you and need you in their lives.

When you set aside time for a task, for exercise or anything else, let your colleagues and family know your schedule wherever appropriate. I'm a writer and I know a lot of writers. They're a wonderful group. However, one thing I have little patience for are those few who say they don't have time to write. No one has time to write. We *make* and *take* time for that which is important to us. If it's not important enough for us to make it happen, it won't happen.

Remember me? Four jobs, a wife and kids? I've written and published more than twenty books in the last few years and I know a bunch of authors who are much more prolific. We all have twenty-four hours in a day. Allocate time. It's there for (almost) everyone.

I say *almost*, because I've been lucky and I've been privileged and I've always written. I say *almost* because there are undoubtedly people who face difficulties, disabilities and a lack of privilege. However, if you are taking the time to talk about writing and you aren't writing? Then forget the free pass. Just about anybody can make time to write at least one book.

The Diving Bell and the Butterfly is a book written by Jean-Dominique Bauby. After a catastrophic stroke and a coma, the former editor could only move his left eye. Writing was painstaking but, by tracking eye movement, he dictated the book that would prove a lasting legacy for everyone. Puts effort in perspective, doesn't it?

Make time.
Take time.
Guard your time.

Do the no excuses thing.

The Power of No

I hope you are expert at something or you're working toward that goal. One expert I know is a brilliant graphic designer. Once in a while, a potential client contacts him about a project. They'll say, "This is a really easy one that won't take you long so get this finished and back to me right away. I'm on a tight deadline. Oh, and since it's so easy, can I get a discount, too?" Sometimes they even add, "Or make it free and I'll give you exposure." A person can die from that kind of exposure.

Amateurs are often very confident folks. That confidence is misplaced. The term for this phenomenon is the Dunning-Kruger effect. People who know less about a subject are often more confident when they speak on that subject. They don't know the complexities or gloss over them. They are full of easy solutions that won't work. If you are an amateur at something, leave the complexities to the pros.

The professional has his or her own schedule and many clients to appease. To the above query, the answer has to be, "No, you can't get it fast, cheap and free." As a professional, guard your time well. You know how long it takes for you to accomplish a task at which you are expert. Estimate accordingly and don't let non-experts tell you otherwise. Stay on *your* schedule.

I used to be at my clinic at all hours, morning and night. One client from long ago was always late. I needed the money so I stayed and he received treatment. I didn't complain so I trained him to push me around. After multiple appointments missed, it began to gnaw at me. When I finally did confront him on his rude behavior, he did not return. I was surprised to find I didn't miss the money. My stress plummeted and I found other clients who respected me and my time.

When I had children, I realized how much time I was wasting by hanging out at the clinic and dealing with administrivia. I got more efficient in dealing with paperwork. I wanted to get home to cuddle my babies so I set my work hours strictly and I stuck to them.

Occasionally, I encounter resistance from clients. "I booked for half an hour, but I can stay for an hour," or, "I'll take the last appointment of the day so it won't matter if I'm late." My answer to the former is, "I have plans right after this so we can schedule for an hour next time." My answer to the latter is, "Yes, it matters. Don't be late. If I'm not here when you arrive, you'll have to work on yourself."

If a client doesn't show up at the expected time, they must reschedule. If they make a habit of not showing up, they're charged for my time. In rare unfortunate cases, I have to suggest the offenders find a new therapist. When I made this transition to respecting my time, I have to admit, it was easy to say no. I had kids at home and I wanted to get back to them. To those who tried to insist on me altering my schedule, I simply replied, "I have to pick up my kids from daycare."

That's a solid reason, but now that my kids are older, my time and stress management policies remain the same. Is a childless worker's time worth no less? Whether you have kids at home or not, *all* our time is important.

Time is life.
Do the important things.

You Are Not a Robot

Staying late at work is a point of pride with some people. They want their car to be the last one in the parking lot. They think it makes them more valuable to the company or even more valuable as a human being. These folks outstay everyone. Rarely do they actually outwork everyone. In other words, they need to get a life outside of work. You can work hard or long, but it's unlikely you'll manage both.

What this behavior tells me is that the offenders are inefficient. Perhaps they're spending too much time cruising Facebook during work hours. Maybe they really are working too hard, propelled by fear and desperation. Could be they should reevaluate what they're doing so they become more effective.

You know those cooking shows where an angry chef is the terror of the kitchen? He shouts, bangs pots, swears and bullies his staff. Some of that nonsense is for the cameras, I know. However, it's not all fake. His behavior is somehow excused because that is the culture of the restaurant kitchen. I don't like watching those shows. I hate to see people getting pushed around, especially when it's for the entertainment of the bully and the audience. Unfortunately, some think that's the way to act because they see it on TV.

I heard another (calmer) chef say something wonderful. He said that all those screaming tantrums indicate that the chronically angry chef has failed to train his staff properly. It was the chef's own failure that got the drama going. In a better run restaurant, no one is throwing a hissy fit. When's the last time you went to a diner and saw a short order cook panicking because he's got a busy restaurant? It doesn't happen. (And don't take your cues for workplace behavior from Gordon Ramsey, no matter what you do.)

How does this apply to your workday?

Organize tasks and expectations on human time, not robot time. I know a lot about robots. I know you aren't one. You know you aren't a robot, right?

Parkinson's Law is that work expands to fill the time allotted.

Do the unexpected thing and break this law.

Never be late again

I once attended a meeting where a woman burst in the door late and agitated. Embarrassed at being late, she made quite a show of how stressed she was. She didn't apologize for being late. Instead, she detailed how angry she was because she had to share the road. While she portrayed herself as the victim, it was clear to all present that she had indulged in road rage.

Her anger was so over the top that it robbed time from the purpose of the meeting. I suggested, rather pointedly, that she might enjoy the ride to the next meeting if she left five minutes earlier. If worry about lateness is your stress (or you are causing stress to others in this way) set your watch ahead or set alarms on your phone to tell you when you should prepare to leave. Depart when you should, leaving enough time for slow traffic.

The larger issue is how this angry person saw the world. Clearly, she was the star of her own movie and the rest of us hadn't read her script. We were supposed to get off the road and stay out of her way.

Newsflash:
You are the extra in everyone else's movie.

Try a new mantra:
If you aren't ten minutes early, you're late.

Do the respectful thing.

Rules to Live Better By

Here are two principles I find very useful:

1. The Pareto Principle AKA The 80/20 Rule

You get 80% of your results from 20% of your efforts. You've surely heard that before. Do you use it?

Let's make this example concrete. For freelancers: Do you spend most of your time on the fruitful 20% of your customer base? Or are you spending most of your time (and aggravation) chasing the 80% of clients who use your service or product rarely and are more difficult to deal with?

Make it even more concrete: Bad customers are sucking your time, your life, your enjoyment and your profit. They're also taking you away from good customers who like you, trust you and are a joy to work with. Is it time to fire clients? Is it time to focus your efforts on the people you enjoy working with?

Since stress management is really time and energy management, you can apply the Pareto Principle to many aspects of your life. Too often we make the mistake of trying to appeal to everyone. Human nature being what it is, you simply cannot help everyone. No one solution is right for every individual. Sometimes, despite our best efforts, personalities clash. If everyone likes you, you're probably doing something wrong (or you're doing nothing).

2. The Law of Diminishing Returns

Suppose you are facing a challenge. You put more and more effort into the project. You invest precious time and energy. At some point, you get less out of it than you put in. Lots of gurus will tell you to keep pushing and pushing. What if it's smarter to stop or change strategies?

This is my favorite guideline. The Law of Diminishing Returns is a lifesaver. It saves so much time to evaluate tasks this way. Unfortunately, it's not how a lot of people think. One time I was working out at a gym when I spotted six guys moving in a pack from machine to machine. They took turns so, as one guy exercised, the others watched. There was no intensity to what they were doing. As I passed one of them, he bragged, "We've been in this gym for five hours!"

But how much of that time was spent actually exercising? How much energy was expended and how much time was wasted? Time spent does not equal energy expended. Those guys at the gym had invested too much time and received very little in return for their efforts.

That cousin you argue with about politics at Thanksgiving? If he didn't change his mind in the last three years, he's not going to change his mind now. Why are you sitting next to him, spoiling for a fight and wasting your time? Are you sticking with a broken relationship that was once good and now sucks because you think, if I just try harder everything will be okay?

Good coaches know the body has limits. They aren't there simply to scream, "Faster! More! Rah! Rah! Rah!" Bad coaches break bodies. Do not push yourself to the breaking point.

This common mistake arises from a flaw in our cultural programming. We are often taught that if we simply work harder everything will be better. This is not true if you're working at the wrong thing.

What's more effective?

Listen to your body. Listen to feedback. Measure responses. Examine your time and energy expenditure with a cold clinical eye. If the rewards are getting smaller with more effort, it's time to change that losing game.

Do the things that pay (psychologically, emotionally and monetarily).

The Quickest To Done

When you have several projects on the go at once, which should you work on first?

My answer is always the same. It's *not* necessarily the project you're most passionate about. I suggest you complete the project that is closest to done.

You can't gain experience, learn from mistakes and improve if you don't get projects done and out in front of others. For instance, I have little patience for traditional publishing anymore because it takes so long to get books to market when you use intermediaries. I'm part of a group of writers who have what promises to be a very helpful book. The people who would benefit from that book are going to have to wait. It's for a traditional publisher and there are a lot of cats to herd. Cats don't take well to herding. While we wait to hear from publishers on that book, I'll publish this book (and hope it helps the same audience.)

That's one of the reasons I love writing this book. I control when it gets out to an audience. Establishing some level of control of your fate is a key to stress management. You get where you're going faster and make fewer stops along the way when you drive your own vehicle.

Your calendar is your friend. Use it to mark your days, track your progress and get stuff done.

Do the damn thing!

Never Be Late Again

When I was a kid, our teachers showed us grainy films featuring a little boy with tragic teeth. He wore a red plaid shirt and a buzzcut. The object of the movie was to get us organized. One thing has always stuck with me. If you lay out your clothes for the next day, you'll get going faster in the morning.

It's a simple thing, but a lot of time is wasted when you're searching the sock drawer for a matching pair of argyles and wondering where your clean shirts went.

**Do the thing that won't make you late
(or make you wear your clothes inside out,
backwards and mismatched.)**

Lower Goals Get You Started

High expectations are great. They can also feel overwhelming and relentless. Try a mind trick dedicated runners use.

On cold winter mornings when they aren't feeling up to a 5K, runners who love the warmth of their beds fool themselves. They get up by telling themselves, "I'll just do one mile. I'll be back in a hot shower in no time."

Once they're out, they'll probably end up doing more than a mile. Maybe they'll do two or five or ten. Getting started is the toughest part.

As I write today, I'm within three thousand words of completing the first draft of this book. To meet my production deadline, I had to write roughly 1,600 words a day. I already had all my research notes lined up and an outline to work from. That made slipping into writing mode easier. I had my *why*, *where*, and *when* taken care of. I didn't have to think long about *what* I was going to write each day. I just had to focus on *how* I was going to write.

Then I set a modest goal. This is not the sort of advice you usually get from gurus, I know. I don't aspire to be a guru, though. My modest goal is to help you manage your stress while you get unfrozen and move on to greater success. Set a modest goal and you won't be intimidated. Most important, you'll get started.

For most of us, success doesn't require a Herculean effort of the blow-the-doors-off variety. All that's required is that you get the modest goals done. Your advantage is that, though many people share your goals, they aren't getting started. They're stuck in loops of procrastination, shame and misapplied effort. Mostly, the people you'll beat to the finish line won't jump into the race at all.

This book is full of tips to make small course corrections to get things on track. My goal is not to make your life story the subject of a made-for-TV melodrama. The goal is to get procrastinators moving in the right direction. You can do everything you want without tension headaches, grinding your teeth and screaming.

Huge goals and massive expectations can grind you down. The internet seems to be full of "success teachers" who berate their students, bullying them for not working hard enough. Well, enough of that. Let's just get stuff done without the drama.

Many of us have to write things in the course of our work, so let's talk about writing for a moment. Specifically, how I met the goal of writing this book with less stress.

At first, I tackled the easiest chapters and used notes from stress management classes I'd taught. I moved on to topics I cover often with clients. Once I started getting ahead on my word count, I set less daunting goals. Sometimes, the least intimidating goals give you such momentum from the start that you hate to quit. As a result, I had quite a few days where I wrote 3,000 words and even had several days where I wrote more than 5,000 words for the first draft.

By setting modest goals and getting ahead of them, I wrote the first draft to this book in 30 days despite having to take several days off for injury and illness. (For several days, my hands hurt so much I had to dictate instead of type.)

I've written several novels the same way: consistent effort, not heroic effort. Why? Because, for me, the hardest part is settling down to start the work. It's a common problem, but modest goals get things started and rolling. Consistency gets things done.

Many people dream of doing things they'll never get around to. They don't need to dream more. They need to wake up and jump in. Often, you'll learn what you need to know by doing.

Do the small things consistently.

SECTION III

PAIN MANAGEMENT

The Long & Short on Pain

We've discussed the relationships among stress, energy and pain. We've talked a lot about time and energy management to combat stress. It's time to delve into pain management strategies that may be of assistance.

Warning

If you have a physical pain that is undiagnosed, consult a health professional. Mild to moderate pain can often be dealt with by a variety of holistic strategies. However, severe pain requires more proactive medical intervention. All pain should be investigated and diagnosed before you try non-medicinal strategies to alleviate pain. Ask your doctor if the strategies in this section are right for you before implementing any of them. You are responsible for your health. Get help when needed.

**Listen to your body and do the things
that cause you less pain in the long run.**

Is Your Pain Serious?

If the doctor says, "You're going to feel a little pinch," whatever they're up to is probably going to hurt. I use the word *pain*, but only because I want you to avoid it during treatment. As a massage therapist, I help people every day with a variety of painful conditions.

Before you try massage therapy, here's what you need to know about alleviating stress and pain using manual therapies. Where appropriate, manual therapies can be very helpful with pain and stress that is mild to moderate. When pain and stress become severe, however, it's much harder to relax, stretch and exercise your way out of trouble. Consulting a physician, exploring other treatment options and employing pharmaceuticals may be more appropriate than manual therapy.

I ask patients to rate their pain on a scale from one to ten to gauge improvement. I want to find out how much of a miracle I've performed by the end of the session. Quantifying improvement subjectively demonstrates the value of treatment to clients. I'm also exploring how severe their pain is for clinical reasons.

Recently a woman came to me with pain in her calf that was bad enough to make her limp. As she described her pain and how it came on, I assessed her problem. Instead of treating her, I referred her to the nearest hospital for further investigation. I suspected she had a clot in her leg. Massage Therapy would not help a deep vein thrombosis.

**All massage therapists get one rule instilled in them
from the beginning of their training:
If in doubt, refer out.
That advice applies to you, too.**

Suppose you have a tight muscle in your neck or a strained shoulder. Rate your pain on a scale of one to ten. Discomfort is mild to moderate pain. Pain in the moderate to severe range requires a higher level of investigation to rule out more serious issues. In other words, call the doc and get a medical diagnosis. I am constantly amazed by people who put up with pain for a long time before seeking treatment. Minor health problems become major issues when left untreated.

Got a pain you've never felt before in your abdomen? Call the doc. Don't rely on crystals, angels or positive thinking to will your way out of a medical problem. Not sure what's going on but it feels bad? Call the doc or call an ambulance. Don't screw around.

Do *not* google your symptoms. Dr. Google will convince you that your mild case of tennis elbow is arm cancer. Dr. Google is an expert in misinformation and worst case scenarios. I repeat, don't listen to Dr. Google! He will often mislead you and he'll only increase your stress.

Do the consultative thing.

Pain Tolerance and Your Brain

Let's dispense with the myth of high pain tolerance. A lot of people are very proud of their so-called high pain tolerance. It's sort of a misconception that requires some nuance to explain. It's not some sort of biological numbness that makes you superhuman or at least tougher than the average bear. With rare exceptions, we all have pretty much the same sensitive physiology when it comes to sensing what's going on in our environment. Pain means danger so, barring some medications or neurological impairment, we generally feel the same when poked with a sharp stick.

Those few people who really don't feel pain end up hurting themselves a lot, by the way. It's true that there are cases of nerve damage and nerve impingements where pain is deadened. (If you think of part of your body as, "deadened," high pain tolerance suddenly doesn't sound so attractive, does it?)

I say high pain tolerance is *sort of* a myth because, beyond the physiological outliers, there are people who appear to be less bothered by pain. However, I mean that quite literally. It's more psychological than physiological. Given the same pain stimulus, they'll feel just as much pain as anyone else physically. The difference is, those with high pain tolerance attach less significance to what they are sensing.

My mother was one such person. She hated taking painkillers so much that she went without any kind of numbing agents during dental procedures. Imagine the sound of the dentist drilling into your teeth and digging toward nerves. Now imagine getting that done to you without any medication. My mother preferred the pain.

Painkillers get a bad rap from purists. Some think medication should be avoided at all costs. Beware of that "all cost" kind of thinking. There are downsides to some medications and those issues should be discussed with your doctor or pharmacist. I sure wish my mom, an OR nurse, hadn't been quite so afraid to take pain medications as she was dying. Mom refused pain medication during her cancer treatment until the very end of her life. Martyrdom and suffering is no virtue if it can be avoided. Tolerating needless pain doesn't make you stronger.

Do the painless thing where appropriate.

Stop the Collapse

Now that we've got the caveats and warnings out of the way, let's talk about where so much of our stress and pain is coming from. We hear a lot about heart disease, cancer and the growing epidemic of diabetes. The media pummels us with warnings of terrorist attacks daily, but that sad fate is extremely unlikely compared to the clear, present and ordinary dangers we face daily. We often worry, but we also worry about the wrong things.

Let's find a solution for something you can act on immediately. One of the more ordinary stressors is ubiquitous, real and causes a lot of pain. It's the root of a plethora of musculoskeletal problems that quietly, consistently and insidiously contribute to your stress. I'm talking about our relationship to gravity.

Most people in North America sit too much. Particularly since the design flaw that is suburban sprawl was introduced to the design of our cities, we drive everywhere. We sit for hours at a time as our necks crane forward to peer at screens.

In postural analysis, this is called a collapsed posture (where the muscles at the front of your body are stronger than those at the back). Look around any coffeeshop. See all that slumping? See how heads crane forward to talk to each other so they can make themselves heard in noisy public places? Start looking for it and you'll find the phenomenon everywhere.

There are easy strategies to improve your energy by changing suboptimal postures. You can avoid pain and cut off headaches related to postural dysfunction with a few simple tricks.

Good posture is not an exaggerated military stance where your shoulders are thrown back and your chest is puffed up. Good posture takes less effort than that.

Instead, try this: Stand. Picture a string attached to the middle of your sternum. Imagine that string pulling straight up. If you have a collapsed posture where the muscles in the front of your body are working too hard, you'll discover your weight shifts back toward your heels. Neat, huh?

Now imagine there is a string at the crown of your head. Imagine it pulling straight up. Did your head just get repositioned? Relax your shoulders. It may feel uncomfortable and unfamiliar at first, but this is good posture.

Sit at your desk. Imagine that same string at the crown of your head pulling straight up every time you hit the delete button. The delete button is your cue to delete your maladaptive posture. You'll sit straighter and that has benefits you probably weren't taught in school. When you sit straighter, you are able to breathe deeper. Each deep breath is a message to your nervous system that signals there is no reason to be nervous. Good posture is calming. Delete the slump, feel better and enjoy having less stress on your body and mind.

Do the delete button thing and correct your posture.

A Pull Not a Pain

One of the easiest ways to reduce your stress is to stretch regularly. When you do it right, it feels good.

Begin by rotating your joints at your ankles, knees, hips, shoulders and neck. Pull lightly on your wrists and fingers, rotating the joints gently. Before getting into the earnest stretching, warm up with some light calisthenics or running on the spot. You need to raise your temperature. No need for a thermometer, just move enough to get a light sweat going.

Once you have a little perspiration, you can safely begin to enjoy stretching. Watch a cat wake up from a nap and you will observe a perfect example of the enjoyment in stretching. A good stretch should not be torture.

A good stretch always feels like a pull, not a pain.

The question of how long to hold a stretch is somewhat controversial. A few years ago, one study even suggested that stretching is bad for you. This is a prime example of why the public should not pay attention to small preliminary studies. Pilot studies are often reported by the media as if science has come to a final conclusion on the subject. Science doesn't do that (or at least it takes its sweet time coming to conclusions).

If you stretch properly, you will not hurt yourself. You may even prevent injury. A 10 to 15 second stretch is probably too short. Thirty seconds per stretch seems optimal for most people. After that, the law of diminishing returns starts to kick in. I suggest usually 30 seconds. That will encourage you to stretch without the excuse that it takes too much time.

You probably know what to do already. If you don't, get some personal instruction. It's beyond the scope of this book to go through all the many yoga poses and physiotherapy variations to get you flexible and bendy. If you stretch without pain, you will stretch well. Be gentle with yourself. Have fun. Listen to music while you stretch. Breathe deeply to relax into a deeper stretch if you like but be sure to do it at your speed. Everyone is different. If your tissue is tighter than that of a stretch buddy, do not compete with him or her. This is your song and you will sing it the way only you can sing it.

I studied martial arts for many years. I found that the stretching I did before a workout prepared me for the challenges ahead and prevented injury. The stretches I did after a full workout seemed to increase my flexibility.

Take the time to stretch, enjoy it, and you will want to make it a regular part of your day. If you rate your stress on a scale of 1 to 10 before and after stretching, I suspect you will be pleasantly surprised how effective this one stress management tip can be.

Do the surprising thing.

Cut the Tension

Take a moment to look in the mirror. Is one shoulder higher than the other? Do your shoulders roll forward? This is pretty easy to spot even if you aren't very aware of your posture. What you're seeing is an asymmetry in the way your muscles function. Some muscles are shorter than they ought to be. Others are long and tight as your body argues with gravity.

Tight muscle takes up energy and makes you less efficient. Poor posture can lead to pain, less energy and more stress because your musculature is in a constant tug of war.

Starter solution:
Move more.

Intermediate solution:
Try the two tennis balls in a sock solution on the following page.

Best solution:
Yoga

Ask a friend to join you and take a few yoga classes to see how you like it. It's for all ages and promotes symmetry, stretching and strengthening. Regular yoga practice leads to less stress, more energy and less pain. If you can't afford yoga or it's not available where you are, there's still YouTube and DVDs. Try it out and see if yoga is for you.

Do the bendy thing.

The Tennis Ball Solution

I suggest this tool to several clients every day. As long as you don't bruise easily or have a condition where a bit of pressure into thick muscle will hurt you, you're going to love this. When your muscles are tense and you're looking for a quick fix, there's an easy solution you can take anywhere. This one could change your life immediately for the better.

1. Take two tennis balls and put them in a sock, preferably a long one. Bunch the tennis balls together so they are touching and keep them together with a bit of string or an elastic.

2. Put the balls between your back and the wall. If you use a long sock, you'll have something to hold on to so you won't drop the balls as often.

3. With your heels close to the wall, position the balls on either side of your spine. Work your way up and down the spine.

4. Press in gently (don't torture yourself) and don't put pressure directly over the spine. Don't use anything harder than a tennis ball in this position and don't lay on the floor where you can't control the pressure.

5. You may feel discomfort as you press in. Discomfort is fine, pain is not. If the discomfort dissipates after a few seconds, you're using the right pressure in the right spot. If it increases, stop. If it persists, move on to another area or stop. You're in control of the tennis balls. Use your best judgment so you don't bruise yourself.

6. Remember, as you do it and when you're done, it should feel *good*. The muscle will be less tense, more relaxed and softer.

7. After the muscle is released from tension or spasm and relaxed, stretching may be more enjoyable, too.

Do the thing that's both a treatment and a treat.

The Red Light Reflex

I learned about the Red Light Reflex many years ago in massage training. Poke somebody with a stick and your muscles will contract. This metaphorical stick could be be a stalled car, bad posture, a pain or a problem. It's true for psychological stress or physical injury. Under stress, humans tighten up their muscles. Short musculature can lead to pain, loss of function, loss of range of motion and discomfort. Let's relax instead.

Massage therapy, yoga, meditation and numerous techniques in this guide can help you can address the Red Light Reflex. Reduced stress translates to less muscle becoming unnecessarily tight.

Inducing a relaxation response and reducing muscle tension is the Green Light Reflex.

Do the Green Light Thing.

Manual Therapy

There are many treatments for the effects of stress and pain. As a manual therapist[1], I can reliably bring down your pain and stress, make the muscles in your shoulders feel like a gel and make you a safer driver by increasing the range of motion in your neck.

Frequently clients emerge from a session saying, "I feel so much better! It's like magic!"

No. It's not magic. I trained and took numerous continuing education courses to develop the skills that I apply to make positive changes (primarily to affect the neuromyodermal body systems).

Massage therapy is the physics that *feels* like magic.

Manual therapy assists with a long list of chronic and short-term injuries and issues. In a typical week, I help people seeking relaxation, rehabilitate sports injuries and massage people facing end of life issues. In the week that I wrote this chapter I treated two patients suffering jaw pain, a fibromyalgia client and numerous people with shoulder injuries, low back issues, headaches and wrist pain.

Many clients request deep tissue massage. I gladly deliver deep work but if that's not your thing, don't worry. Professional therapists are not cookie cutters who go to the same depth all the time. Your individual tissue tension, tolerance, treatment plan and medical conditions will vary. Therefore, the pressure used should be tailored to your individual needs.

I often run into people who think that a good massage requires a "no pain, no gain" mentality. Actually, the reverse is generally true. If the pressure goes too deep too quickly, you will tighten up. (*See Red Light Reflex.*)

In most treatments, we're trying to soften and relax tight muscles, not shorten them. Some clients require a lighter touch. Others wish to deepen the pressure and we can do that as their tissue tension improves.

Here's the formal definition of my scope of practice: *Massage Therapy is the assessment of the soft tissue and joints of the body and the treatment and prevention of physical dysfunction and pain of the soft tissues and joints by manipulation to develop, maintain, rehabilitate or augment physical function, or relieve pain.*[2]

I would add that our aim is also wellness enhancement. I'm sure that was in a draft of the legislation governing my profession somewhere along the line. I don't know what happened to that key element. In short, most people feel much better after receiving a massage, especially by a professional.[3]

To find a massage therapist near you, ask for a referral from your friends. Styles of bodywork vary widely. Get a recommendation from a friend in your area. Word of mouth is usually the best way to find the therapist who will be the best fit for your needs.

Do the massage therapy thing.

[1]My title is RMT, as in Registered Massage Therapist. I prefer the terms manual therapist or biomechanic because, historically, massage has associations that do not represent the highest professional therapeutic intent. (Fortunately, that is slowly fading.) Sometimes it feels like the word *massage* also oversimplifies what I do to help people.

[2]Source: College of Massage Therapists of Ontario website, Standards of Practice.

[3]Despite how medical and professional our goals, we must never lose sight of the fact that many people just want to relax during a massage. Not every session is a medical "treatment" per se. Unless indicated, I don't take every client's blood pressure before a treatment, for instance. That act in the massage therapy context sets up an illness dynamic rather than one of wellness. Anxiety around the test itself causes an increase in blood pressure that is needless among the vast majority of my clientele. I'm not here to torture you or make you feel paranoid about your health. I'm here to help.

The Daily Do

There are many manual treatments and exercise regimens designed to improve our lives, decrease stress and pain and increase vitality. Whatever your treatment of choice (e.g. massage therapy, chiropractic, physiotherapy, personal training), think of your time in the office as a helpful course correction. You don't expect to make major changes that will affect your stress, pain and energy by doing something once. Once a month in the gym doesn't build biceps that bulge.

If you have appendicitis, you only have to get that surgery once. It's removed. Stress, pain and energy management require *ongoing* treatment. Everything you do each day adds or subtracts from your quality of life and vitality. The daily zip through the fast food drive-through will take its toll. The 10,000 steps you make sure you get today boosts your health quotient.

Look to the causes. Stay vigilant for signs your stress is building. Adjust your days accordingly and work on doing more of the healthy things than the unhealthy things. The things we do regularly will determine how our lives are lived. Ours is not a consequence-free dimension, no matter how much we wish that were so.

Do the Daily Do. That is the thing.

Happy Distractions

Television shows and movies have the capacity to carry us off with emotion. I love being swept away by fiction. When I'm feeling down, I watch movies that are easy on the nerves. Though I write apocalyptic books, sometimes it's nice to watch a show where you know everything is going to work out fine.

I had thought this a somewhat frivolous stress management strategy. Then I remembered the terminal patients I've worked with over the years who used distraction as a powerful pain and stress management tool. Losing yourself in a narrative that is not your own is a great idea when you need to get away from what ails you.

After my wife and I had children, I was surprised to find how sensitive I'd become to certain movies. For instance, I won't watch a movie that features sexual assault. I've heard *A Time to Kill* is a good movie but it's not for my tender sensibilities. Even though my fiction is suspenseful, I've never watched any of those CSI shows. It's too close to the real thing. I prefer my violence to be of the fantastic and relatively unlikely variety.

So, what to watch? When my kids were little, I watched *SpongeBob Squarepants* and *iCarly* with them. As a grown man who had kids pretty late in life, I had to ask myself why I liked watching this sort of stuff. I didn't have to think too hard. I've read all of Stephen King's fiction. I have a pretty dark sense of humor. However, what I loved about G-rated shows was that little or nothing was at stake.

We have a steady diet of bad news (See the chapter called *Combat Sensory Overload* for more on that.) When you're under stress, be careful of what you're sticking in your head.

I've always been a movie buff so there are plenty more movies I like than the list I'll give you below. Tastes vary so I won't even attempt a comprehensive list. However, I erred on the side of safe distraction where you'll finish happy, safe and triumphant. If you're looking for goofy fun and feel-good stuff, here are my top go-to movies and TV shows.

1. The Princess Bride

2. NewsRadio

3. The Karate Kid

4. Brooklyn Nine-Nine

5. It's a Mad, Mad, Mad, Mad World

6. How To Succeed in Business Without Really Trying

7. Love Actually

8. Ferris Bueller's Day Off

9. The Fantastic Mr. Fox

10. Groundhog Day

11. Happy Feet

12. Say Anything

13. Up

14. The Secret Life of Walter Mitty

15. High Fidelity

16. Toy Story

17. Shrek

18. School of Rock

19. The 40 Year Old Virgin

20. Finding Forrester

21. Wonder Boys

Enjoy the happy distractions. If it's strong enough to ease pain, it'll do the same for stress.

Bite Your Tongue

A client shared a cool trick with me recently. She had a habit of cranking up the tension in her jaw while at work. When she was working on detailed tasks she noticed the muscles of her jaw shortened and tightened as her stress climbed. Then her jaw began to ache.

If you have Temporomandibular Joint Dysfunction (TMD, commonly mislabeled TMJ), you're probably familiar with this pattern of exacerbation. My client found that if she stuck her tongue between her teeth while she worked, she stopped clenching her jaw. Clenching meant biting and she got reminded quickly if she tensed up.

There are massage therapy treatments for TMD but, before I use them, my first question to these clients is, "Do you chew gum?" If so, stop and see if your symptoms abate.

Here are a few more tricks for a tight jaw:

1. Awareness is often enough to get you to relax any muscle. The trick isn't getting it to relax. It's upping the awareness so you can relax. Use a frequent cue, like checking the time, getting to the bottom of a page or each time you touch your face.

Odd note: People touch their faces a lot. To avoid infection, we probably shouldn't touch our faces so much, but we do. To adjust our glasses, scratch an itch, rub our eyes, yawn or as a self-soothing gesture, we are face-touching machines. Might as well use that behavior as a useful reminder for something positive, right?

2. Jaw still tight? Try putting the palms of your hands on either side of your face. This is one of those natural self-soothing gestures. In this case, we want to achieve something mechanical. When your jaw is tight, position your hands so the little ridge at the top of your palm rests just above the bone of the jawline. Gently — really gently — let the weight of your arms pull straight down. This is a subtle move. No need to press in or press down. Let the muscles of your face and jaw relax with this little reminder. Be gentle with yourself for best results.

3. If your jaw is still tight after using the above tips and tricks, it's time to drag out the big gun: the Isometric Jaw Release.

It's really simple. Put your fist beneath your chin. Bringing your teeth just slightly apart, press your jaw into your fist for fifteen to twenty seconds. Your fist is there to provide gentle resistance. Don't punch yourself in the jaw.

When you take your fist away, feel for a slight lengthening in your face. That's the relevant jaw muscles releasing and lengthening. Use a cue (like checking the time etc.,...) and you'll get that jaw uncranked.

Do the page flip thing for important information about TMD.

TMD Trouble

Temporomandibular joint dysfunction is a common issue. For most people, it's their dentist who will first notice damage to the teeth related to TMD. Stress, dental issues and sleep apnea may also contribute to jaw clenching and pain. If you have a sleep disorder where you are clenching your jaw in your sleep, the strategies I've listed here won't help. Ask your dentist if a night guard is right for you.

Over the last few years, I've noticed a lot of clients list that they possess a night guard to protect their teeth. I always ask the annoying question, "Do you use it?"

Frequently they reply, "No, I keep it in my nightstand."

"I don't think it's so powerful that it works like that." (I'm funny.)

Check with your dentist about the fitting to make sure it's as comfortable as possible. There is sometimes an adjustment period where you feel like you're drooling more in your sleep. Get past that, use it and protect your teeth.

Do the night guard thing.

Where's Your Head?

We live in a very desk-oriented world. We sit too much and yes, as you've probably already heard, sitting is the new smoking. As a writer, it's a problem with which I have struggled. I used to skim over alarmist stories in the media about the dangers of a sedentary lifestyle. To pursue my writing career, I knew I would continue to be sedentary. I wasn't interested in reading scary articles that provided no solutions. However there are ways to combat the problems of the sedentary.

Let's start with postural stress and then move on to more energetic strategies to get you back into gravity, even at work.

When we walk, we are always on the verge of falling. Standing and walking is an ongoing conversation with gravity. Our muscles, ligaments and nervous systems become finely tuned to keep up our end of the conversation so we don't fall on our faces.

Don't believe me? Try this awareness exercise:

1. Stand. Place your hands on the back of your thighs. The muscles beneath your hands are the hamstrings.

2. Bring your head forward as far as you can.

3. Do you feel your hamstrings contracting? You will.

What's happening there?

As you bring your head forward — a common problem that makes the muscles in your neck and upper back contract — your hamstrings are contracting, too. That's your body doing its job correctly. It's compensating for the weight of your head coming forward. Your body is contracting all that neck and shoulder muscle to try to bring your head back so it's better balanced over your spine.

Similarly, when you bring your head forward, your hamstrings contract to try to keep your conversation with gravity going. By that I mean your hamstrings contract so you don't fall over like a tree and — *timber!* — break your face on the sidewalk.

When a runner comes to me and complains that their hamstrings are too tight, the first thing I look for is a head posture that is too far forward. If their head is too far forward, I work on their neck and head posture before I touch their hamstrings. The hamstrings are innocent in this argument with gravity. Those leg muscles are just doing their job to protect your face.

Most articles about sedentary lifestyles focus on getting you up and moving more. (We'll get to that.) But first, let's make sure your head is close to optimal, sitting or standing.

When you correct postural stresses, you spare yourself a lot of discomfort. Postural problems that are left unchecked eventually turn to pain. When pain goes up, energy goes down and stress goes up.

Let's avoid all that stress, shall we? On the next page, you'll see how to check your head posture so this theory becomes practical.

Do the practical thing.

Do You Have a Head Forward Posture?

This will give you a quick idea of where your head is at.

Feel that little rounded bone directly behind your ear? That's called the mastoid process. It should be lined up with the seam of your shirt across the top of your shoulder. If your head is forward of that seam, you've got muscles in your back and legs that are working harder than they need to.

There are many ways to address postural distortions. Entire bodywork systems (and lots of books and practitioners) address a multitude of maladies related to posture. Matrix Repatterning, the Mckenzie Method, Rolfing, Egoscue and Muscle Balance & Functional Development are a few of the big ones to explore.

A good start is to revisit the crown string technique, covered in the chapter titled, *Stop the Collapse*. Also consider yoga or get a massage. Use cues for postural corrections to reinforce your efforts to get your head on straight.

For best results, review the relevant chapters and take action on those suggestions.

Cue yourself to do the most useful things more often.

The Eye Exam Question

When a client comes to me with a head forward posture, my first question is, "When was your last eye exam?"

You can do all the postural correction you want. If your eyeglass prescription is weak, your head will be pulled forward every time as you peer at your computer screen.

**Look for causes before treating symptoms.
Do the optometry thing on a regular basis.**

The Power Move

We all sit so much, bending toward computer screens and cell phones, that our heads are carried in a forward posture and our shoulders slump. Later in this book, I will give you several suggestions to address problems of ergonomics, standing desks and inactivity. First, let me share with you a simple postural solution that applies to almost everyone.

When you clench your teeth your neck muscles become short and tense. For every inch that your head comes forward, your shoulder and neck muscles tighten to try to bring the weight of your head back over your spine.

When your massage therapist palpates your shoulders, this is one of the signs we're looking for. Feel the muscles of your shoulders yourself, squeezing the muscles between your thumb and your first two fingers. Squeeze the muscles across the top of your shoulders (the upper fibers of the trapezius). Feel how hard they are? Now let's work on an easy solution.

When I was a young and naïve therapist, I would suggest exercises to consolidate the gains my patients would get from massage therapy. I thought in terms of sets and reps. I was trained to give a variety of remedial exercises as homework where appropriate. I still suggest remedial exercise, but now I have a much higher compliance rate among those I serve. Here's how:

1. As you take a deep breath in, you're going to squeeze your shoulders toward your ears, feeling the full contraction of the muscles involved. It's a simple shoulder shrug.

2. Feel the full contraction of the muscle across the top of your shoulders. Then feel the full release as your shoulders drop toward your hips on the exhale. No need to hold the contraction or to hold your breath. Feel both phases: the contraction and relaxation of muscle.

3. What you're doing is retraining muscle at the top your shoulders to be more relaxed all the time.

Just like when you squeeze your hand into a fist, it feels more relaxed afterward, right? That's what you are replicating here. After a skeletal muscle reaches full contraction, it gets a little longer in the relaxation phase. Enjoy the feeling. (If, for whatever reason, an exercise causes you pain, stop and get the problem addressed with professional assistance.)

4. Congratulations. You've just performed a shoulder shrug. There's not much that's easier than that.

I don't suggest sets and reps so much anymore. Cues, like performing a shoulder shrug each time you pass a doorway, reinforces the desired action more often. In case you're jumping around this book, dipping in to find something useful, you'll find more suggestions for cues in the chapter *Hack a Better Life*.

Now that we're getting your head where it should be, relaxing your shoulders and making you more comfortable, let's get on with getting you out of your chair more.

**You only have to do the shoulder shrug thing once each time you go through a doorway.
Consistency is more important than enthusiasm.**

Do the Scap Slide

It is amazing how little it can take to change your posture and change how you feel. When I find my neck and shoulders are tensing, I take a deep breath and imagine my shoulder blades sliding down my back. I don't even have to force it.

Try the Scapular Slide:

Don't arch your back or hold your breath. Just imagine your shoulder blades sliding down your back. That's all there is to it.

What did you feel? Did you sense change in the weight distribution in your feet? Did you head come back slightly? Did your shoulders drop? Are you more relaxed?

Do the Scap Slide thing. It's nifty.

You and Your Desk

**I once attended a posture workshop in which someone asked the instructor
what kind of chair is best.
"None," came the stern reply.**

Let's begin with the desk you probably have now. Is it an ergonomic setup? If you are not sure, look to your forearms and thighs. When you sit at your desk, are your thighs and forearms parallel with the floor? Is your body turned one way while your head is twisted to one side to look at the monitor? Are you sore at the end of a work day? If so, a professional ergonomic assessment might be in order.

However, don't rely solely on proper ergonomics to prevent injury. An optimal desk arrangement is not enough. Whether your desk hurts you or not is not entirely dependent on ergonomics. It's also about the body you bring to the desk.

Regular exercise and taking care of yourself are still necessary. Ergonomics cannot outwit poor body mechanics and muscles that are deconditioned. Even with a perfect ergonomic arrangement, someone in poor condition will still feel the ill effects of sitting at a desk for too long.

If you work for a large enough company, they may pay for a desk that rises and lowers to accommodate sitting and standing. For the lone entrepreneur, such desks may be prohibitively expensive. The cheapest such desk I've found is, as of this writing, available from IKEA. There are also rigs that sit atop a regular desk that raise and lower to mimic a height adjustable desk.

I have seen a number of improvised standing desks using lap desks on top of desks, boxes or bookcases. If you can manage it, this may be an excellent low cost solution. Make sure the surfaces you put your computer on are solid and secure so it doesn't all fall to the ground with a cataclysmic crash. There are standing desks made of cardboard that are much less expensive than those made of wood and metal but I can't speak to how long they will last.

**Let's delve deeper into some workplace options on the next page.
Do the things you can do.**

Move More

Sitting at a desk all day is hard on your body and your heart. We've known that sitting for long periods is bad for some time. I was very frustrated to read the research given that I was often working at a desk so many hours a day. *Okay, I get it,* I thought. *Sitting is bad for me, but what do I do about it?*

Numerous strategies have emerged. Here are my suggestions to cut down on the amount of time you sit:

1. Consider a treadmill desk (AKA a tread desk.) There are many on the market. I built one out of a manual treadmill I bought for $100. I bought a piece of wood, drilled some holes in it and used zip ties to secure it to the treadmill handles. With very minimal carpentry, it was a simple matter to put my wireless keyboard atop the board and walk while I worked.

This was not a perfect solution for me. I found that I could surf the web while I walked but I could not write while walking. Since I spent so much time at my desk, I still needed to find more solutions to complement the treadmill desk.

2. My next move was to purchase an exercycle that sits beneath my desk. I got more of a workout on the exercycle than I did with the treadmill desk but, once again, it was too awkward to use the machine while I wrote. For me, it was only useful for passive tasks, not active work. Still, it was an improvement on the treadmill desk because I found I could cycle for much longer while at my keyboard.

3. Next, I tried a Swiss ball. I found the Swiss ball was great for my back. The ball encourages you to engage your core muscles. Sitting on a ball makes you aware of all the little adjustments your body is making in its conversation with gravity. That's the pro.

The cons? If you get a Swiss ball, make sure it's high enough for your desk. If you sit too low it feels like you're a little kid trying to eat at the grownup table. The other issue with my Swiss Ball was that it rolled away every time I stood.

My solution was to get a chair that accommodates a Swiss ball. It's basically a hoop in which the Swiss ball sits, complete with backrest. The chair is on wheels, but it did not roll away every time I stood up. I found I could work on the Swiss ball chair for extended periods. Eventually, though, it made my butt hurt.

As I write this, it seems the tread desk has become a passing fad. A lot of people can't seem to get used to walking and typing. I have no doubt the treadmill desk has its champions but are they outliers? Even the standing desk may be too much of a challenge for an eight-hour workday. I suggest that if you cannot handle a tread desk, alternating among your options is the most realistic and practical approach. It could be that treadmill desks would be more popular but their cost makes them less ubiquitous than they might otherwise be.

If you do not enjoy standing all day, you could try a mat to make standing for long periods more pleasant. There are spongy mats, often used by checkout cashiers and in kitchens in front of the sink. There is also a new mat coming out that has a rounded center and edges on which to stand. By varying your stances, you can incorporate stretching and extend the time you can stand comfortably. Alternatively, you might try wearing more comfortable shoes or going barefoot.

Find the solutions that are practical for you and mix and match. Whenever you can, decrease the amount of time you spend sitting. After all the talk of treadmills, standing desks and other gizmos, the consensus seems to have moved on to so-called, "dynamic sitting." That means try a bunch of sitting and standing strategies so you get up and move often. There are apps you can program to encourage you to get up from your chair often. In bettering your health, make your computer an ally instead of the enemy.

Do the frequent movement thing.

How to Make Sure You Move

One sure low tech solution to sedentary work is a water bottle. Bring a big water bottle to the office. If the bottle is transparent so you can see the water level, use a marker to denote the hours of the day. Drink water so you keep up with the time.

As you drink from your water bottle throughout the day you'll definitely need to get up a lot. When you go to the bathroom, take another lap or two around the office for good measure.

For a high tech solution, consider using a Fitbit, Garmin or similar pedometer to encourage you to get at least 10,000 steps a day.

**High or low tech,
do the non-sedentary thing.**

About High Heels

High heels were designed to make the calf contract for aesthetic purposes. In other words, those shoes make your legs look great! I love the look of high heeled shoes. However, from a bodywork, energy and health perspective? Don't. Just don't. They're sexy, yes. They must be for so many people to insist on suffering the torture of wearing them.

High heels shorten the Achilles tendon. Tight toe boxes (the front of the shoe) mash your toes together and put too much pressure on the forefoot. Meanwhile, your back muscles are working harder so you don't fall forward since your center of gravity is radically changed. High heels are uncomfortable foot prisons that mess with the natural dynamics of your musculature.

If you must wear them (or you just really want to) wear them for shorter periods. Wear sneakers to get to work and put the foot prisons on after you get to the party or the office.

And guys? Wear a three-inch stiletto pump once and try walking around. It will make you more compassionate to women. Or maybe you'll find high heels are your thing. From a bodyworker's perspective, I still can't recommend high heel shoes to anyone.

When it comes to footwear, do the comfortable thing.

Pain Tolerance and Your Brain

Pain has two more interesting aspects: body noise and denial. Both are very important to stress management. Body noise can heighten your stress but denial can delay appropriate treatment.

Doctors describe body noise as the odd ache or pain that has no clinical significance. For instance, when you kneel or bend and you hear a loud pop in your knees? Sometimes that's a tendon snapping over a bony prominence or it could be a normal part of the dynamics of your joints. Such a noise is called an auscultation. Unless and until it's painful, it's not considered pathological.

How does body noise relate to stress?

Nervous people sometimes get in a loop of thoughts that make them more nervous. I've had clients who take the most innocuous vague sign as the tolling of a mournful bell. "Is it cancer?" is their first question for everything.

I don't mock them. I have personally suffered health anxiety on several occasions. When I studied anatomy, the amazing dynamics of human physiology made me think there must surely be a God. Then I studied pathology and I was sure there must be a devil. Med Student syndrome is a common problem and it's not just for med students. First responders and anyone who works in a hospital or a funeral home may go through phases where they think, "I'm really not eating enough kale! Look at all the terrible things that can happen! Should I wear a helmet to bed?"

For me, I can go through a cycle of pain and anxiety in which I begin to suspect that the odd ache or pain is significant. Stress makes my every ache or pain worse. It's happened to me enough over the years that I now recognize the pattern. I ease the symptoms by reminding myself that, oh, there it is again and I've been in this mindset before. Such feelings are my cue to step back, observe and retool my responses.

For instance, a few years ago, I was convinced I had liver or bowel cancer. Abdominal pain stalked me. It was alarming and persistent. I visited my doctor and changed my diet. Things got worse.

I saw my doctor again and went through two exploratory procedures. Given my pain and its location, a colonoscopy was appropriate to rule out a host of problems that could debilitate or kill me. I'm happy to report that I didn't have cancer. I had a spasmodic colon. Don't worry. That's not the point or punchline to this story.

Here's the interesting thing: as soon as I had a definitive diagnosis that ruled out one of my greatest fears (i.e. cancer) the pain that had plagued me for months was gone within a couple of days. My worries exacerbated the spasms in my colon. As soon as I knew I was in no danger, my symptoms disappeared. You could say the happy outcome of the test cured me of my pain.

I learned a lot from that experience. Mainly, I realized the value of stress management and relaxation. My health issues made me appreciate the importance of what I do. I had underestimated how stress can make pain worse. Manage stress better and your pain will often diminish.

But what if my pain isn't just body noise? That would be Denial with a capital D. Time for a short but important message about Denial.

Avoid delusions.
Do the real thing.

About Denial

Don't assume that every ache and pain is merely body noise. Get it checked out. (Remember, if in doubt, refer out?)

I know. Sometimes it seems like navigating the balance between not worrying too much and being careless is a trip along a high wire in a high wind. However, the solutions are simple. Get a consult and get checked out with regular physicals. When changes occur, ask your doc what he or she thinks.

While I waited in constant gnawing pain for my colonoscopy to be scheduled, I visited several practitioners (and one quack). I was desperate for relief of my pain. However, I didn't allow alternative treatments and dietary experiments to delay evaluation by my doctors.

When you allow denial and/or fear to paralyze you from seeking assistance, you may be making a bigger problem for yourself. For instance, after the age of 50, colon cancer instances increase. If it's caught early, you won't die. Get regular checkups. You'll experience much less stress, fear and premature death by being proactive.

Sorry. I don't believe in using scare tactics and this chapter wasn't meant to do that. However, seeing things as they are is an important stress management strategy. Delusion should be confined to the fiction we read. Denial is not a healthy policy.

Do the medical thing.

Eliminate the Cause

I work with many people to help them decrease their stress and get out of pain. When I look at what solutions work (and what doesn't work), those strategies and tactics don't take place in a vacuum. I can lay out a dozen remedies and recipes for alleviating stress but succeeding in stress management is not just about tricks and tips. It's about lessening the number of stresses you have to manage.

**Focus on causes,
not just signs and symptoms.**

Recently, a fellow came to me complaining of pain and tension in his shoulders. I'd never seen trapezius muscles so tense that they bulged like thick cables. I worked on him for half an hour using every trick I knew. When I was done, I palpated the upper fibers of the trapezius again. I can usually turn shoulder tissue into a malleable gel in short order. I'd characterize the change after this treatment as a moderate release. He wasn't satisfied. He wanted all the tension gone immediately.

I replied that he should try the tennis ball trick daily (See *The Tennis Ball Solution*). I talked about posture, ergonomics and using cues to exercise his way out of all the tension he experienced.

He stared at me pugnaciously. "Is that all you can do?"

I confess to being slightly annoyed. "If you want to make a major change, you're going to have make major changes, like stretching the tissue daily and eliminating the causes. I can't combat the habits of a lifetime in half an hour. No one can." Borrowing a line from Scotty on the original *Star Trek*, I added, "I canna change the laws of physics, Jim."

Consider what you can edit out of your life. What good habits could you adopt to get you closer to your goals? What bad habits need to be dumped? Eliminate the cause of your stress and you'll never have to manage it again.

**Decrease the causes of your troubles where you can.
Do the physics thing.**

Self-medication

If you're dealing with pain or stress, it can be tempting to self-medicate. People try to numb their pain in all sorts of ways. Maybe you do it with drugs, food or alcohol. For instance, many people with low back pain use liquor to ease their symptoms, especially if they are elderly or don't have an insurance plan that covers the expense of pain medications.

I urge you not to self-medicate. See your doctor and get a proper prescription. Consult your pharmacist to ensure you are avoiding medications that conflict with other prescriptions or dietary choices.

Perhaps the most common self-medication is food. Under stress, we crave sugar, salt and fat. We crave the chemical combinations calculated to be most addictive by the food industry (and I'm not just talking about the fast food industry). For instance, caffeine does not improve the taste of a soft drink. Caffeine is included because it's addictive. Use the drug advisedly.

For more on this, check out *Salt, Sugar, Fat* by Michael Moss in the Further Resources section.

Do the medical thing, not the self-medicating thing.

Heat or Ice for Injury?

Heat and ice packs are cheap low-risk solutions to minor pain or injury when applied correctly. There are a few straightforward caveats, though:

Any application of heat or ice the patient doesn't want is not the way to go. For instance, insisting on using ice when it causes the injured person to contract in pain is less than helpful. The application of heat or ice should feel relieving.

Don't put heat on top of inflammation (i.e. where an area is hot, red, painful or swollen.) Heat can assist with soothing muscle spasm. Ice can contribute to spasm and stiffness.

When someone sprains an ankle, it seems everyone has picked up the RICE advice by now: rest, ice, compress, elevate. For minor injuries, that's still the way to go. Do not leave it on for extended periods. You don't want to burn or freeze the skin.

When you use heat or ice, apply it for a maximum of ten minutes. Remove it for five to ten minutes then repeat as necessary if you feel it's helpful.

Don't trap heat by lying directly on top of a heating pad.

Don't use heat or ice on a person who cannot communicate that they've had enough.

Don't use heat or ice on someone whose circulatory system or nervous system is compromised to the point that they cannot sense damage done to the skin.

Heat and ice packs can be soothing and helpful but they aren't miracles. If any problem gets worse or doesn't go away, of course, consult a physician.

Do the thing that applies to you.

Cannabis

I haven't seen another stress management book discuss drugs that are not traditionally prescribed. That's why we need to talk about it.

Marijuana is so popular a drug that, between the time I write this and the time you read it, it might be legal for recreational use in yet another state. It will soon be legalized in Canada. The polls are in and people are more and more friendly to the idea that cannabis should be taken out of the hands of criminals, legalized and taxed for medicinal or recreational use.

The research is in, too. (It's been in since the Nixon administration, actually.) The alarmist message of *Reefer Madness* is dead. Fans of putting non-violent drug offenders in jail (i.e. the Prison-Industrial Complex) regularly show how out of touch they are by supporting the enforcement of outdated laws with junk science. Worse, the application of those laws is unambiguously racist. White guys caught with marijuana frequently get warnings. Black and brown people go to jail. People who partake of cannabis are frequently called lazy losers in the media. However, from Ben Franklin to Carl Sagan and many US presidents, a long list of overachievers who have used the drug recreationally.

I'd prefer a conversation with a stoner over a drunk any day. I *hate* talking with people who are drunk. If you drink or smoke, you have no business objecting to marijuana. It is literally impossible to overdose on marijuana. As comedian Joe Rogan often asks, if it's so dangerous, "where are the bodies?" There aren't any. As drugs go, it's quite safe.

Outlawing cannabis was a triumph of lobbying by the pulp and paper industry who wanted to sell wood and couldn't compete with hemp. Blame William Randolph Hearst for manufactured hysteria that fed all the misinformation we've been fed for decades. Lobbyists from the tobacco and liquor industries did not want that competition, either.

So, in short, "History! Science! Facts!"

We've established that marijuana is not nearly as harmful as propaganda would have us believe. Still, it is not for everyone.

Though cannabis is a very common drug with a long history, its use is not always addressed rationally on both sides of the issue. (See the tightrope on evenhandedness I'm trying to walk here?)

Cannabis is a popular self-medication among those suffering stress and pain. It has demonstrated usefulness with some medical conditions. Despite its benign nature, cannabis is *not* for everybody all the time. Since the brain is still developing until the age of 25, recreational cannabis use is not for children and young adults. **If you're not an adult over 25, cannabis is not for you.**

Please be careful how you self-medicate. If you're under stress, cannabis might not be the best choice. Exercise and/or prescription drugs might be better. If you have a history of psycho-emotional problems, cannabis may make you worse. "Contraindicated," in med speak. As in, *not for you.*

I know someone who suffers crippling social anxiety. He self-medicated with marijuana and it did not help him. It made things worse. Compounding the problem, using cannabis delayed him from seeking proper medical attention for what turned out to be a serious mental health issue.

I mentioned Duncan Trussell once before in the chapter about getting the clutter out of your life. It's time to paraphrase him again. In a podcast interview with Joe Rogan on *The Joe Rogan Experience*, Trussell said marijuana can give you a harsh dose of truth if you are in a bad place in your life. If you're basically happy, marijuana can be pleasant. If you have a lot of debt, the truth of your circumstance and your failings can hit like a hammer.

If you have a history of mental health issues, don't assume you can self-medicate without supervision. Consult a physician. The world is changing with regard to cannabis. Individual mileage (and dosage) does vary.

**Do the thing that helps you.
The thing that helps you might
not be what helps others.**

You and Your Devices

When I was very young, a teacher gave my class a hard time about our computer files. "I see the disorganization of your minds on your computer desktop," he declared.

He was pretty rude and it wasn't fair. No one had trained us in how to organize computer files so we could find them quickly and work with them efficiently. It was a little like getting a quiz on the rules of croquet without ever playing the game.

Here are a few things to keep in mind when you're decluttering your desktop:

1. Name your files carefully and keep the titles short and linear.

2. Files have extensions that indicate the date on which they were created. However, it's quicker to spot files if you include a date. For files I don't anticipate keeping a long time, I still add the month and day so I can find it quickly. For instance, *Groceries 1109* is a shopping list for November 9. If I expect to keep the file longer, say, notes for a speech, I'd label the file: *Stress Speech 110917*. Simple, right? However, there are a lot of cluttered desktops out there.

3. Use folders, starting with broad categories first and then subfolders that fit that category. For instance, *Family Pics* might be a broad folder and then subcategories could include, *Christmas 2015* or *Summer Vacation 2015*.

4. Use your bookmarks menu. Break out the broad categories just as you would with desktop folders, according to the usefulness of the websites you want to remember (e.g. Marketing, Publicity, Vacation spots, Money Management, Hobby etc.) Bookmarks save time. You'll not only be able to find what you want to keep on hand, you won't slow your computer down by keeping a bunch of tabs open. You tell yourself you'll get back to that thing you want to research but in the meantime your computer is struggling to work with the drag of your demands.

5. Periodically, clean out your computer of the files you no longer need. Regular maintenance reduces the computer's response time so

it speeds you up, too. This probably falls under the category of something you know and have forgotten to do or you've been meaning to get to it. Easy enough. Figure out how often you're willing to run a disk diagnostic and set the task in your Google calendar.

6. Backup your information. All computer drives fail eventually and there's never a convenient time for that to occur. There are a lot of options you can use to backup your data: Dropbox, OneDrive, iCloud, external drives and memory sticks. Choose two and use them to avoid heartache. Regular backups save days, weeks, months or years of work and memories when your computer dies. (Save a small percentage of your income each month to replace your computer when it eventually dies.)

Let's talk more about doing the productive thing.

SECTION IV
ENERGY MANAGEMENT

Schedule Energy, Not Just Time

As a freelancer with four jobs to cover, my life is a jigsaw. I've got a busy family with kids who do a lot of things. They often need rides to those things. My Google calendar looks like a patchwork quilt. I use a central calendar (linked to my phone). When you take a few minutes to fill out a calendar to stay organized, time management is actually pretty easy. Time management is doable and easy to measure.

As a writer, I get more work done early in the morning and late in the evening. I suggest you schedule high productivity tasks for when you're most energetic. Four in the afternoon is a low energy time for me. I avoid tasks that demand much from me at that time. That's a great opportunity to do dishes, listen to podcasts or take a power nap. (If you're interested in napping productively, check out the chapter called *Power Nap Tricks*.)

One way I manipulate my body so I'm sharper is to avoid eating low nutrient foods. Sweet and salty high calorie carbs may give me a short burst of energy. When the sugar crash comes I want to lie down and rest. To stay really sharp, I go on short fasts.

We are bombarded with commercial messages that we need constantly fuel our bodies to get them to function at all. Unfortunately, most fast food won't help you and we're actually more mentally acute on empty stomachs. Our hunter-gatherer ancestors went about their life or death tasks best on empty stomachs, too, so refraining from constant feeding makes sense, doesn't it? For most people (barring metabolic health issues) we don't really have to fortify our bodies with massive feasts to start the day. Unless your health is severely compromised, you've got plenty of fat reserves to see you through a short fast.

There are numerous ways we stimulate our bodies and manage our energy. I use caffeine and power naps. I time tasks to my biorhythm. In *Think and Grow Rich*, Napoleon Hill even manipulated his energy by foregoing sex. He found he could put his heightened energy to use for business purposes. I don't recommend this practice. Healthy sex is a birthright and a stress reliever. I don't advocate foregoing the best fun there is to boost a number on a spreadsheet.

Be aware of your biorhythms. Are you a night owl? I used to be one, too. Then I discovered the power of an earlier bedtime and getting up early. (Check out the 5 A.M. Miracle under Podcasts in the Resources Section of this book for more strategies to get more stuff done while everyone else sleeps.)

Do the energy management thing.

Energy Management Part I

My friend and podcast guru Dave Jackson (Schoolofpodcasting.com) often says, "If you have the *why*, you will figure out any *how*."

Do you know *why* you want and need to achieve a particular goal? Find your why.

If you're a regular reader of self-help literature or listen to a lot of podcasts oriented toward goal-setting for success, you'll hear a lot about lofty goals that tend to be outlier-oriented. There are many passionate people who honestly believe outstanding success is for everyone. They may not think you've made it until your house is bigger and you've got a three-car garage. There are also cynics speaking into microphones who know that it's easier to sell a book or a webinar by promising the world.

Perhaps you're heard of the so-called laws of attraction? That's otherwise known as Wishing Hard. *The Secret* has pretty wrapping paper but that box of wishes is empty. Don't get out the crayons to draw dream maps of where you plan to put the piano-shaped pool behind your mansion. It would be much more useful to use that butcher paper to create a flow chart for your product development.

**Make your goals realistic, short-term
and easy to plug into your calendar.**

I'm not saying you can't manage your life to great success. I'm saying that success looks different to everyone. Your plan might be a vague notion of fame and fortune that we have to delve into deeper in order to make concrete. Maybe your goal right now is to feed your kids and sleep more without stress turning you into an insomniac. Don't let others judge your goals. They are yours and yours alone.

To make your priorities a reality, let's talk more about working backwards from your goals.

Do the personal thing.

Energy Management Part II

I've written in general terms about goal-setting and figuring out how to break it down. Let's get into *your* specifics.

Stress Management Key:

Work backwards from your goal with a calendar and a calculator by your side. I've talked about goal-setting and using a calendar, but it's using the *calculator* that makes all your efforts concrete.

1. Figure out what you need to achieve. That is: what *value* will you provide others with the work you love? What challenge will you solve for yourself or what problem will you help your clients solve?

2. Selling something? How much can you charge for the valuable product or service you provide? (Back up to the previous chapter to work this out with clear eyes.)

3. How much money do you need to pay your monthly bills? Use a calculator. Don't guesstimate. Take everything into account to determine your minimum income needs at current levels.

4. How much income are you making now or what time can you commit to put toward your goal? What can you do to make up the difference? How much money do you have to have in the bank to safely commit all your resources to an entrepreneurial enterprise?

Got your answers to those questions ready? If not, go ahead, I'll wait.

5. Make this exercise as concrete as possible, given your current resources, talents and allies. Calculate all the expenses before you project what income you might expect. Stay conservative in your tallies. When you know what it costs to provide your services, figure out what profit margin you should set that won't drive you out of the market. Take industry standards as a rough guide. Your competitors may be charging too little or too much or they may have different costs. You have to do your own math to make sure you're positioned to be profitable.

About goals for
selling products and services:

If you can't charge more for your product or service, you'll need to sell a lot of it. If you got out a calculator to perform this exercise, you can figure out a lot of things. For instance, you can work out how long it will take to pay off your credit cards at your current rate of pay.

If your time is limited and you're charging premium fees for a high-end service, all the elements will have to be in place to sell that service. If you're offering a hundred dollar massage session of which you only do a few a day, those towels better be plush and the work must be excellent. If you can charge more for your product or service, you don't need to produce and sell as many teddy bears, manage as many clients or fix as many toilets (or whatever value proposition you're offering the world).

When all your calculations are complete, do you still have a viable proposition for your target customers? Keeping in mind that everybody wants everything better, cheaper and yesterday, what variables might you change to make your value proposition more viable? Don't go by your gut feeling. Go by your calculator.

What about using the time machine
for personal goals?

As with all life management projects, work backward from the goal and start filling your calendar. For instance, if it's a weight problem you've put your mind to, you know your target weight and how long it will take you to achieve that goal if you commit to losing 1.5 to 2 pounds each week.

If your aim is to solve money woes, you'll soon know exactly how much time and energy you'll have to commit to meet your goals and pay off the bills. (See the Chapter on poverty, debt and credit cards to bring down those bills.)

Using your calendar to plan backward instead of forward gives you a timeline with solid daily commitments to the goal. Quantify your goals, costs and commitments by numbers as much as possible. That's the power of the time machine combined with a calculator.

Do the calculated thing.

Hot baths and Haircuts

The best suggestion I can make about leisure activities is that you do them.

Everywhere I look, I see people rushing around. Sometimes I can see that if I glance in a mirror. I am reluctant to take a night off. It is my wife who insists we take a vacation each summer and she's always right. I come back from vacations rejuvenated and full of new ideas I want to act on. Time off is never really time off for me. I write fiction so I suck up all the non-fiction around me and use it when I can.

A lot of people can't afford to take a vacation. I'm not suggesting a trip to Fiji is mandatory for mental health (although, if you can manage it, that would probably be wonderful). As a family, our vacation plans are often modest but no less satisfying. We can't always fit an expensive trip into our time or money budget. Here are a few suggestions if a big ticket trip isn't feasible.

1. Go camping. It's much cheaper than hotels.

2. Stay with friends. Last summer we visited friends in Chicago. We had one of the best vacations of our lives. We took a cheap train ride, saved a lot of money on hotels, reconnected with friends and made new ones. (Chicago is awesome. Go see the Blue Man Group if you can.)

3. Day trips. Within a day's drive there are zoos and aquaria, tourist attractions and plenty of sights to see. Take a day off and see what you've been missing close to home.

4. Staycations. We often ignore tourist attractions in our own cities. We miss out on the allure of destinations right under our noses. If nothing else, we can stay home, unplug the phone, curl up with a book and act like we're a thousand miles away with no pressing responsibilities.

5. Get out of the house, take a walk and get social. Be with friends. Change the conversation from, "What have I got to do next?"

259

to, "How are you and what's going on in your life?" Have a life outside of work. Do not allow yourself to be defined by what you do to make money.

6. Exercise. When you really can't take a vacation, you need to exercise more to blow off steam and stress. I'm not suggesting that you exercise as a replacement for a vacation or that you should only exercise as often as you vacation. We should all exercise every day.

On the busiest days, some quiet time in a hot bath may be all the time you can spare. You can, and should, do that little, certainly.

Treat yourself when you can. When you get your hair done, say yes to the hair washing, the scalp massage, the hot towel and the pedicure. Wear the fancy underwear that makes you feel you're the hero of a movie. Go to bed early. Pamper yourself. Get a massage. Look for the opportunities to do the little things daily that make you feel your best. Even dogs get treats so treat yourself at least as well as you treat your dog.

If you're resistant to vacations, try shutting off the phones and unplugging from media or internet addictions. Most of us are not as indispensable as we'd care to think. Being too available all the time is a prescription for building stress.

Not everything demanding your attention is urgent. Unless you're a brain surgeon on call, surely something can wait. When someone tells me they can't take a vacation due to poverty, I get that. When someone tells me they can't take a vacation because their office would fall apart without them, that's a poorly run office that needs reorganization.

What do these people do when they get sick? Do they come into the office to make sure everyone else gets the flu, too? Treat yourself as important because you are.

Only robots work without vacations. Don't be a robot. Do the human and humane thing.

Active relaxation

Someone out there is raising a hand to object.

"Yes? You, in the back. What have you got to say?" (As if I didn't know.)

"You tell us to plan our work but I can't get on board with planning my relaxation. Planning is the opposite of relaxation."

"I understand, and you're wrong," he said gently. Here's why:

Unplanned relaxation leads to more stress.

If you've been to Disney World, you know how crazy busy it can be. There are many things you can do to make that trip more pleasant. For instance, arrive early for when the gate opens. Also, purchase the unauthorized guides to Disney destinations. The guide will show you the shortcuts and most efficient routes so you spend less time in line and more time enjoying the park.

If you go to Disney and decide you're going to wander around, you'll see and enjoy less than half of what informed visitors see. The ones who plan the pattern of which ride to go to for maximum fun exposure don't waste so much time baking in the sun. Don't end up like the irritated visitors I saw. An older woman and her grown daughter yelled at each other as they tried to decide what to do next.

The other reason you need to plan your relaxation time is applicable to any day off, anywhere. If you begin the day telling yourself this is your day off, you're in for a relaxing time whatever you do. If you tell yourself you will do some work and you procrastinate, you may still get a day off but it will feel a bit miserable and aimless. Any time you spend thinking you should be elsewhere increases stress.

If I plan at the beginning of the day to write but I keep putting it off, the tyranny of an unplanned day has two negative effects:

1. I don't get any writing done.

2. I tell myself I'll write sometime later so I feel the pressure of procrastination and, eventually, guilt because I didn't get to it.

When you are working, work. When you are relaxing, relax. Don't mix up the two and you'll be happier on your days off. If you don't plan your commitment to relaxation, you won't get to experience it.

Do the forward-thinking thing.

Improve Your Skills

We often don't appreciate how ignorant we are until we begin to learn new skills and information. You can go to school, of course. There are other opportunities to expand our knowledge, too. When you want to know how to do anything, turn to the internet.

One acquaintance of mine wanted to teach online courses but didn't know where to start. That turned out to be a minor obstacle. He subscribed to a course on how to set up courses. Using the templates provided by his online mentors, he has churned out several successful courses.

I know a person who had no graphic design training. She learned how to use Photoshop so well that she started up a graphic design business.

Another friend started up a sharp little side hustle refurbishing old electric guitars in his basement. He learned how to accomplish every repair by watching YouTube videos.

There are more formal sites to learn from than YouTube, of course. If you want to learn new skills that make you a better job prospect, check out Phlearn, Lynda.com and The Great Courses.

Are you of a more philosophical bent? Try the School of Life.

A creation of Alain de Botton, author of *Status Anxiety*, among others, *School of Life* is a YouTube channel that will clue you in on history's big ideas. Consider it a great overview of the great thinkers of history. These short videos make learning relevant to our lives.

Read Alain de Botton's book, *How Proust Can Change Your Life*. If I fail to help you in this book, maybe Alain de Botton will. To find out more about the author, go to his website.

Do the online learning thing.

Difficult People Part I

As I write this, I'm dealing with a sociopath. In the normal course of one of my jobs, someone asked a question. I gave them an answer and, I swear on little kittens and all that's holy, it was an innocuous answer. My reply was intended to inform, not to offend. I can't provide the transcript for obvious reasons, but I assure you, the email reply I received would make you either horrified or snort laugh.

The person became instantly enraged. There was nothing in my typical friendly customer service answer that would offend a normal person. This was not a normal person. She told me I was nasty and hostile. She said I overreacted to her question and (in a not so subtle threat his superiors would not appreciate) mentioned that her husband is a cop.

Uh-huh. Not normal.

A number of blistering replies came to mind. I wasn't hostile until she went nuts. Then I began to compose a number of unsubtle replies about projection, persecution complexes and insanity.

So, how did I really deal with Mrs. Crazypants in the end? I didn't. Instead, I passed her correspondence over to my partner to evaluate who was rude and who was not. He composed a kind reply which basically said, "Hey, we don't stand for inappropriate behavior and we won't be the ones to help you from now on. Best of luck elsewhere."

In the end, you have to feel sorry for some people and their families. Every day must be filled with arguments, crying jags and mystification as to why all their friendships are short lived.

Drama is seductive. Psychodrama is some of the sexiest nonsense there is. When someone loses their mind on you like this, it is easy to pull apart what they say, shake out the lies and make them feel bad, wrong and tiny. You've seen it a thousand times in Facebook arguments. Someone states an outrageous opinion and you feel that urge to jump in and correct them on their twenty-seven false assumptions and misinformation.

Next time that happens on Facebook, try this:

1. Write out that scathing reply that cuts to the bone and displays that you have the knowledge they don't. Explain the world to them.

2. Ask yourself, "Feel better?"

3. Ask yourself, "Once I devastate this person with science, facts and erudition, will they change their mind?"

4. If the answer is no — and the answer is almost always no — don't hit publish on your comment.

5. Delete your brilliant reply. Go on about your day, unfettered, knowing that you don't have to sit there waiting for their inane and stubborn comment on your reply.

6. When it happens again, you can probably just skip to Step 5 and go straight to being carefree.

"But," someone is yelling, "if we don't stand up for what's right, everything will stay wrong!" I don't disagree. Turn the page for more on that.

Do the useful things.

Difficult People Part II

Repeat after me:
I do not have to react to everything.

In fact, you can't react to everything and be effective. Remember that other rule I like: There are a million problems in every direction. Pace yourself. Apply your limited energy to the problems you can change.

Here's the weird thing about difficult people: They lash out and soon forget it. You'll remember every inflection of their nasty words forever but they've moved on. They have plenty of people to piss off and there are only so many hours in a day.

So what can you do?

1. If they act mean to everybody, you're not special. You're just in their vicinity. Try not to take it personally because it's not. If you weren't around, they'd be shaking their fists at clouds.

2. They have their reasons for being difficult and it probably has nothing to do with you. Their brains are wired for fight or flight, attack and fear. Maybe they were dropped on their heads as babies or it's a flaw in brain development or they're drunk. None of that is your fault and it's still not your problem. You can't solve that so don't even try. Wish them better days and hang up on that rude phone call. If they call back, don't answer. If they're still a problem, block them. Block them on Twitter. Unfriend rude people on Facebook. You don't owe them anything because you two were once lab partners in 11th grade.

3. Do not try to solve a problem when the problem is another person's personality. You can't solve that for them and, by maintaining contact, you may even enable them. Broken people require the help of professionals and pharmaceuticals. If you aren't a mental health professional, don't engage the crazy. If you are a mental health professional, fall back on your training (and, sorry, only amateurs get to call obnoxious nasty people "crazy.")

4. Difficult people think life is war (See this chapter on that mindset key) and assume the whole world is against them. If the Nasties live long enough, they'll probably succeed in turning the whole world against them. That's their problem. Their problem doesn't have to become yours.

Do the things that make the world a better place.

Do Not Watch Outliers

Some people are go-go-go. I know a guy with a bunch of kids and a demanding job who seems to have endless energy at 49 years old. He's in superhero shape and runs marathons more frequently than is usually advisable for most people. I think he's a wonderful person who accomplishes many great things. He is the envy of many. He's an inspiration!

Here's the problem: he is also an outlier.

I see people compare themselves to others all the time. Writers want fiction author Hugh Howey's success so they, too, can sail the world in a catamaran. They want Stephen King's name recognition though he's been a huge force since before they were born. Investors want to be Warren Buffet so bad that he has fans who eat the same meals as the master of finance. (No, I'm not kidding about that.)

I'm not saying you shouldn't aspire to possess greater energy and do great things, of course. That's why you're reading this book. However, don't put pressure on yourself to win that race two steps out of the gate. People are impatient. Everyone wants to be an overnight success even though that's pretty much a myth. If you compare yourself to outliers, you put your focus in the wrong place. Focus on improving *you*.

The end product is not the work. Every aspiring screenwriter watches one director win the best film of the year award on Oscar night. They wish they could win that measure of fame and fortune. What they don't see is the many years that person worked on the screenplay. They don't see the anguish of rejection and the tough negotiations with studio suits. They don't witness the arguments with the cinematographer that almost came to blows or the sleepless nights sweating financing woes. If you're going to succeed, you have to love the work, not the money you think you're going to get from the work. Yes, love of the work is why millionaires keep working.

Can you become an outlier? You might, but if I said yes to all my readers, that would betray a poor understanding of math. If everyone is an outlier then no one is. I suggest a different strategy to map out your life plan. My plan doesn't depend on winning the fame lottery and hitting fluke home runs by accident. Instead, turn daydreams into work days.

**Turn the page
to do the achievable thing.**

Focus

Do not compare your energy capacity to the unusual. Your goals, your income and your efforts are yours. They are dependent on you and what you can do today. You can increase your capacities and aspire to superhero heights but if that's not where you're at now, you'll get frustrated quickly.

As with managing any resource, you have to be aware of income and outgo to keep your tank full. You're spending energy and you want to make sure you're spending that finite resource on the right things.

As a young massage therapist, for instance, I remember working on ten clients in one day without a break. Each session was a full hour. It was intense but, at the end of that day I felt I'd accomplished something huge. I wondered if this was a new benchmark. What if every day I worked was like this? Could I just work three days a week and take the rest of the time off to work on other projects? That evening, I was tired, but pleasantly so. I went to bed thinking I might have a new standard for how much I could do in a day. I awoke with a sore back and aching hands. Pain changed my mind about working on ten clients a day.

Time management is easy. Energy management is more complex. For instance, if saving the whales is your thing, certainly do that. If you have too many causes to support from limited resources, you're starting a bar fight with too many opponents. Focus your energy to get more done.

Do the focused thing.

The Next Key to Higher Awareness is...
Listening

When you ask a question, always listen for the answer. Many people don't listen. Instead, they're waiting for their turn to speak. You miss out on a lot of social cues and crucial information when you rush ahead without listening. Slow down.

Do the polite thing.

The Myth of Multitasking

There's a very popular idea out there that has, inexplicably, survived a long time. It's called multitasking and, mostly, it doesn't work. If you're doing a task that does not require your full attention, fine. Listen to podcasts or music while you do the dishes. Make the mundane more fun. However, if you're reading, you probably won't take in as much if you're watching television at the same time. Your eyeballs don't work independently like a lizard.

Students, when you're studying, study. Accountants, when you're adding columns of numbers, pay attention. By paying attention, you'll get through tasks more quickly and they'll be performed accurately.

Not to muddy the water too much, but there are people who do seem to perform better with background music. In most cases it's white noise that doesn't really require their attention so it's masking other distractions.

Do the undistracted thing.

**This leads to a larger helpful discussion.
No stress management book is complete without
delving into what's on the next page.**

Email Follies

Machines, apps and gadgets can help you to decrease your stress. However, be sure to use them wisely and well. Machines are supposed to serve us, not the other way around. You don't want to be at the mercy of anyone who can write an email, for instance, so resist the urge to respond like Pavlov's dogs. If you feel you have to jump to reply every time a notification sounds a ring and a ding, you are not in control of your time. You'll be interrupted constantly. Unregulated emails bring on a kind of self-imposed ADD in which you're never focused and some part of your brain is always waiting for the next missive from the ether.

Some suggestions to control stress and time better:

1. Turn off message notifications. Unless you're on call to perform a heart transplant, you don't want or need the tyranny of instant and constant connectivity. You can set your phone to alert you every time someone writes a tweet about you, sends you an email, posts on Facebook or...everything, actually. You can be alerted to *everything*. Don't do that. Keep notifications to the minimum required of you and only during those hours they are really required.

2. Don't keep your phone by your bed. Resist temptation to play a game on your phone at bedtime. Have sex or go to sleep. You don't want your phone by the bed when you wake up, either. People who start answering emails the moment they open their eyes are performing an act that erases the boundary between self and job. You are not your job. You are not a robot. If you don't place limits on when you work, your job owns your life.

3. Boomerang allows you to delay the sending of messages. You can clear your inbox without having to give someone an immediate reply. At first I wasn't clear on how helpful this program would be. I underestimated the feeling of accomplishment of clearing the inbox. You know how Twitter is never done? Email is never done, either, unless you use Boomerang together with #4 below.

4. To manage your email and time better, try using Inbox Pause. It makes your emails arrive in batches at the times of day you deem

appropriate. You'll have fewer interruptions and get more done. Emails *can* wait. If it's an urgent message from a loved one (e.g. your kid is sick and needs to be picked up from school, that's what phones are for.) Use your phone settings to filter out the rest of the world pounding on your virtual door. Do not give your personal phone number to just anybody and everybody.

Do the filtering thing.

Exercise is Medicine

What is the best exercise?
There is no one best exercise.
However, if pressed, I'd say the best exercises
are the ones you will do consistently.

Consult your doctor to make sure you're up for an exercise program before you get moving. There's been a shift in thought recently around weight loss and exercise science. Contrary to the torture marathons you've seen on *The Biggest Loser*, the focus should be more on the kitchen than the gym. (See the next chapter, Food, A Summary.)

If you have a lot of weight to lose, the most recent advice as of this writing (late 2016) is that you should get close to your target weight before embarking on a rigorous exercise program. As Penn Jillette mentions in *Presto!*, you can't outrun your mouth. (See the chapter About Doing Hard Things and The Sunday Afternoon Food Plan for a little more on that.)

There are too many variables to cover every condition, so please do see your doctor first. For some, say those with a heart condition, patients may get the okay to walk downstairs but not upstairs. People with debilitated conditions may have to be more wary of weather conditions (i.e. Not face a stiff wind on the way back from a long walk). Given that you're up to it and have medical clearance, exercise is fine and all you have to do is listen to your body to see how far you can go without injury.

Exercise has been shown to decrease stress. Research suggests that it can be as powerful as anti-depressants in some cases. Maybe your goal is to run a half-marathon but right now you can't run a block. That's fine. Walk and build up to walking and jogging. Bored with walking? Listen to podcasts, music or audiobooks and the time will pass quickly and profitably. If you aren't confident about taking long walks, try going around your block in circles. That way you're never far from home.

You don't have to get an expensive gym membership to exercise. Stairs are everywhere. Use them. A playground has chin up bars and your own bodyweight is plenty of weight to move. All you really need to work out is a good pair of sneakers and a pedometer or a Fitbit to make sure you get at least 10,000 steps a day.

More good news, in *This is Your Do-Over*, author Michael F. Roizon notes that the law of diminishing returns kicks in after 10,000 steps. As someone who has to work hard to squeeze in my 10,000 steps daily, I found that information a bit of a relief.

There are plenty of ways to exercise and you don't have to beat yourself up to benefit. Even by losing a few pounds or increasing your aerobic capacity a little, you will begin to feel better quickly. We were made to move. Studies show that even the very elderly can benefit from strength training. If lifting weights and running isn't your thing, try playing squash, learn yoga or take an aerobics class.

Find the fun and move. Exercise may not lengthen your life significantly. There are many variables that determine life span. If you get hit by a bus, it really won't matter much how many situps you did that morning. However, it's still worth it to enjoy the feeling of a capable body. Exercise is a prescription for a better life with less chance of disability in your old age. To remain active and independent in old age, be active now.

Do the active thing.

For men:

Low testosterone can contribute, among other things, to osteoporosis. All men experience a decline in testosterone over time. Weight loss may help, also. Consult your doctor about testing and treatments.

For women:

Some populations of women are genetically more prone to osteoporosis. Weight bearing exercise from an early age thickens bone and combats onset of thinning bone matrices. Consult your doctor about testing and treatments.

Food, A Summary

Concerned about weight loss? Take any diet in the world that is not a fad. Apply its principles to your life. You will lose weight, at least for a while. Statistically, the odds of losing weight in the long-term are not good.

This isn't a book about dietary guidelines. There are plenty of books about that and they'll cover the material better and in depth. Look to the Resources section for a few suggestions in that regard but don't look to me to step between the Paleo People and the Vegetarians. They'll fight each other until the sun explodes.

I checked the reviews on a bunch of weight loss books and, wow! People really draw up battle lines when it comes to what we should eat! Quote the China Study and some people will jump down your throat and try to feed you grass-fed beef. Are coffee and dark chocolate terrible for you today or has that changed again, too? It's remarkable how much of the research on what we eat is still controversial, isn't it? Affirm that you drink coffee but, if you don't drink it with coconut oil and butter, somebody will yell at you with the heat of vitriol usually reserved for family reunions.

From my research, here's what I feel confident won't change too fast or too soon:

1. We should move more but don't depend on movement alone to burn enough calories to lose significant weight. As Tim Ferriss notes in *The Four-hour Body*, ounces are lost at the gym, pounds are lost in the kitchen.

2. Consume fewer calories. It's the only thing that the majority of scientists agree makes you live longer.

3. Eat a rainbow of multi-colored food to get more nutrients.

4. Eat less processed food because the factory food industry that pumps out addictive confections of salt, sugar and fat are not looking out for your health.

5. Most of what we eat should be plants. Many would say we should eat plants only. Do your own research to decide what tribe you'll join and go scream at someone else. I'm sticking with non-controversial statements here.

6. Maintain a healthy weight and you'll be less susceptible to a long list of diseases that, if I listed them, would make you crave salt, sugar and fat in dangerous quantities. I'm not here to add to your stress and, let's be honest, you've heard all that scary stuff before.

Statistically, if you're trying to lose weight, the odds of long-term success at keeping the weight off are low. Therefore, I suggest a new, different and revolutionary diet strategy:

A. Don't give up because the scale isn't showing you a steady decline in numbers. Weight loss, particularly when you have less to lose, slows. Plateaus are to be expected so resist easy discouragement. Spend less time staring at the scale and more time preparing healthy food choices. That way, change will come eventually whether you stare at the scale or not. If the scale doesn't move at all, consult your doctor for further investigations and possible treatments.

B. Aim for progress, not perfection. One friend tells me his secret is to eat well most of the day most of the time. For him, that means oatmeal for breakfast and a big salad for lunch (without adding sugary salad dressing so that it may as well be a candy bar). He eats dinner around six. Supper typically includes meat but at that time he focuses more on portion control than ingredient control.

C. Don't think of your daily food as a diet. Another friend who lost a lot of weight and has kept it off told me that her winning change came when she stopped dieting. She thinks of her healthy food choices as "the way she lives now."

D. Enjoy your food. Personally, I find that vegetarian food that tries to mimic meat tastes awful. A vegan friend tried to convince me a new product was, "just like having a hot dog!" Nope. It sure wasn't, no matter how many mind tricks and condiments I used.

I find that I do enjoy fruits and vegetables that aren't pretending to be something else. An apple is a perfectly packaged single serving fast food I find energizing. A green smoothie mixed with my NutriBullet doesn't taste bad at all.

As for more elaborate meals, it's all in the preparation. Find a good vegetarian cookbook and experiment. The transition to plant-based eating is for me. My cookbook of choice is *The End of Heart Disease* by Dr. Joel Furhman.

If you're eating healthy but it's food you dislike, you won't keep eating that way. The great news is that, after eating consciously and clean for a short time, I've found I don't enjoy the salty, sugary and fatty food I used to guzzle. My gut biome changed such that the Chinese takeout I used to love gives me insomnia and makes me feel awful.

I experimented with a rare foray into my old eating habits just last night. After a sleepless night, I'm fasting today just to clear out the grease and to feel energized again. My cravings for salt, sugar and fat have decreased immensely and I like using new holes in my belt that reflect my weight loss.

E. Where possible, work with accountability partners to help you with all your goals.

Let's steer away from the food controversies that piss people off so easily and get back to something we're sure of.

Do the peaceful thing.

Food Diary Time Machine

The basis of any food diary is tracking everything you eat. As buff actor Jason Statham once put it, "Write down everything that goes down your throat."

I suggest you try a different kind of food diary. Most people eat and then write down what they ate. Instead, use your diary as a time machine. For optimal results, don't eat your food and then record what you ate. Write down what you will eat for the coming week and stick with that. The best food diary is a food *planner*.

Our brains play tricks on us. One lie we tell ourselves is that we'll get our lives together tomorrow. We are much more optimistic that we'll accomplish tasks when those tasks are set in the future. Sure, I'll get up early each morning! Sure, I'll get to the gym despite the cold. You're more likely to stick to your commitments if you plan ahead and then stick to that plan. Don't imagine that good things will just happen. Make them happen.

Whether your goal is to lose weight, eat healthy or gain weight, you need a plan. Whatever your plan, I suggest you don't think of it as a diet. Diets are fads that come and go. They're restrictive and time limited. I've struggled with eating too much of the wrong things. I'm getting the problem under control now but, if someone asks me if I'm on a diet, I reject the premise. "No. This is just how I live and eat now." I figured out I had to be a different person in order to become that person.

I'm feeling much better now that I'm living and eating in a way that reflects my new conception of myself. I'm sleeping better, focused and feeling better. Whatever journey you are on, I wish you well in becoming the person you want to be.

Do the things that are consistent with the person you want to be.

The Sunday Afternoon Food Plan

Use Sunday afternoon to cook for the week. Chop, cut, cook and freeze your meals ahead of time. Write down each meal, label them and free your mind for the week.

Separate your meals into sealed packages so each meal is ready. This is not the gargantuan task you might think it is. Most people eat the same few dishes over and over. Sit down in your time machine, plan and write out all the healthy meals Future You is going to enjoy in the coming week. Follow through.

You'll save yourself an immense amount of time through the week. You will eliminate many opportunities to make terrible dietary decisions. That not only saves time and gets you on the road to better health, it saves a lot of stress, too. I cook a huge vegetable soup each Sunday that carries me through the week. Apples are ready-made snacks and all I have to do is wash off the packaging nature gave them. I've found eating simple, raw and clean isn't just good for my health. It's a time management strategy.

Aside from cutting out sugar, expensive processed foods and meat, I've let go of dietary habits based on cultural expectations. I don't have to start the day with a big breakfast, for instance. The idea that breakfast is the most important meal of the day has sold a lot of cereal but I doubt it's a biological necessity to eat upon rising. Our history would suggest our genetic makeup is geared to getting up early and functioning well on an empty stomach. Early peoples didn't get up and feast. Humans got up to go hunting and gathering and ate later in the day (if they were lucky.) As I mentioned in About Doing Hard Things, perhaps the best lesson I learned from Penn Jillette's *Presto!* was losing my fear of hunger.

This doesn't mean we have to become grumpy and picky ascetics who never enjoy cake. As Jillette suggests in *Presto!*, his food orgies aren't over. His deviations from plant-based eating are, however, rare and appropriate. In other words, you can still enjoy wedding cake, birthday cake and all the foods you have always enjoyed (but much less often). I used to treat every day as a cheat day from healthy eating. In the moment, it felt good. In the long-term, I was cheating myself.

I grew up with bacon and eggs for breakfast. Greasy foods and tons of sugar, salt and fat was a daily thing. This unhealthy practice was part meal, part celebration, part condolence prize for having to get up and deal with life, I suppose. Food is the connective tissue of our social gatherings. Activities are not broken up by eating. Eating is broken up by activities. It doesn't have to be that way. We can bring the focus back to activity.

And yes, you can have a salad for breakfast and no one will stop you.

"But you can't have salad for breakfast!"

"Why not? Who said so?"

"Um...."

See? Literally no one is policing this. You're free.

If meat is on your menu, Sunday afternoons are a great time to cook up all your chicken breasts for the week. (Vary the seasoning so it doesn't get too repetitive.) I use resealable plastic tubs for some meals. By the end of Sunday afternoon, you're ready for a very efficient and healthy week with no stressing over, "My God! I'm so hungry and what do I eat next? Never mind! I'm tired! Order pizza!"

None are so annoying as the self-righteous and newly converted so I'll stop hammering this topic soon, I promise. Just a couple more quick points. Since changing to eating vegetables and fruit almost exclusively, I don't have to cook so much on Sunday afternoons. Most of what I eat now is raw or quickly heated. I eat so much salad that if I chopped it all up on Sunday it would be spoiled before the end of the week.

For those interested in eating simpler and cleaner, I recommend *Forks Over Knives*. It's both a documentary and a series of books about the health benefits of eating plants. Not only is eating this way helping me lose weight and feel great, I've discovered I'm saving a lot of time and energy.

Do the things that are best for you.

Prep the Week

My wife is one of the most organized people on the planet. If she doesn't know where something is, it's because somebody didn't put the item back where it belongs. When we use up the last of the aluminum foil, we're supposed to add it to the shopping list posted on the fridge. She's a planner and we rarely run out of anything at the last minute. (If we do, it's probably my fault.)

Each Sunday, She Who Must Be Obeyed plans the meals for the family for the week. She notes the ingredients she needs and makes a list of what to stock up on. She's an excellent cook. I'm not. Rather than allow me to accidentally poison our meals, we split kitchen duties. She does the things that require skill and knowledge. I do the cleaning up. It's equitable, plus there's the added benefit that she doesn't have to eat my attempts at cooking.

A lot of people don't seem to plan at all. My evidence is empirical. On civic holidays, most stores and malls close. On the day before and after the closing, those same stores and malls are packed with frantic shoppers. The parking lots are full. The aisles are packed. It's as if there is a hint of panic in the air, the zombie apocalypse has arrived and no one has even one tin of canned peas at the back of their shelves.

Shopping for one or two meals ahead of time is terribly inefficient and leads to more trips to the grocery store. More trips to the grocery store means more bad dietary choices and more money spent.

Grocery stores spread their wares out strategically so you are exposed to more aisles and more impulse shopping opportunities. On the way to the healthy stuff you need to live you will have many opportunities to buy mocha chocolate sprinkled processed crap. Grocers want to make sure you are exposed to plenty of greasy chips and baked goods. That stuff should be called baked bads.

**When you shop for food, don't go when you're hungry.
Make a list, take the list and stick to it.**

If you stick to the outside ring of the grocery store, you'll be exposed to less salty, sugary processed temptation. Spend more time where the raw food is and consume all colors of the rainbow to get more real and more nutrient-dense food. (I'm talking peppers, cruciferous vegetables, apples, carrots and greens, not pretty cereal boxes.)

Do the strategic shopping thing.

Sleep Hygiene

Occasionally, I'm an insomniac. As I mentioned in the previous chapter, I discovered recently how much eating the wrong foods contributed to my sleeplessness. Too much salt, sugar, fat and stimulants kept me awake or gave me punishing indigestion. Eating plants has allowed me to sleep much better. I'm not suggesting that's the solution for you but it would be irresponsible of me not to mention it. I'll give you a bunch of restful strategies below, but the dietary component was the last piece of the puzzle for me.

When insomnia occurs, the next day is pretty much ruined for me. A few days in a row last year I was literally on the brink of tears wishing I could sleep. That's how I got on the "sleep hygiene" bandwagon. I rarely have a bad night's sleep anymore these days. Read on if you have trouble sleeping.

Nobody's exactly sure how much sleep any individual human needs. That's up to you to figure out. Since the invention of the light bulb, the answer to the question, "How much sleep do I need?" is probably, "More than you're currently getting." Sleep deprivation is a form of torture and it's the most common form of torture we suffer. If you feel fatigued regularly and there are no other medical complications, you probably need more sleep.

Part of the problem is that we are overstimulated. We all need adequate rest and recovery time to lessen stress and keep sharp. The sleep deprived forget things and are more prone to health problems. Let's mount our defense against sleeplessness with a quick list of things that help. If you're having a hard time falling asleep and staying asleep, there are simple tricks to try.

1. Bed is for sex and sleep, nothing else.

2. Maybe you aren't tired enough. Get enough exercise, but not too close to bedtime. Exercise late in the day can have a stimulating effect that keeps you awake longer.

3. Avoid stimulants after 4 PM. Cut down or cut out the coffee and caffeine. Look out for hidden sources of caffeine, like tea, sodas,

pain relievers, certain medications, ice cream and chocolate. Even decaf coffee can pack too much of a stimulating punch.

4. Get black out curtains or a sleep mask for the bedroom. Total darkness is better and stimulates the hormonal signals that say to the brain it's sleepy time.

5. Bring down the temperature in your room or use fewer blankets. As your body cools, the body receives the sleep signal. Some people have a warm shower an hour or two before bedtime to get this effect. I've had success with using ice packs to cool the sheets before I crawl into bed. There are even pillows and sheets that stay cool, but they can be a bit expensive.

6. Your computer, phone and TV screens are your enemy if you are staring into the full spectrum light too close to bedtime. There are apps that cut out the blue light emitted from your screen. Those light frequencies signal your brain it's dawn rather than sunset. For a cheap alternative, when I must work late on my computer, I use yellow driving glasses that cost me $7.

7. If you can't sleep, do not lay there and toss and turn hoping sleep will come. After I try to sleep for twenty minutes, I give up and move. Usually, moving to the couch downstairs (that's cooler than bed) does the job. If not, I get up and read a book for a while. You don't want to condition a Pavlovian association in your mind between your bed and the misery of "trying" to fall asleep. There is little more antithetical to getting a good sleep than trying too hard.

8. Turn your alarm clock around so you can't see the glowing red numbers mocking you. If you do wake up in the night, you don't want to mark your frustration with the time boring itself into your brain.

9. Get up early and expose yourself to sunshine as early as you can. This will help establish a healthier sleeping and waking cycle.

10. If you nap during the day (and it's a wonderful thing) keep those naps short. (More on effective napping in the next chapter.)

11. There's been much research into alternative sleep cycles where students have attempted to maximize their productivity by sleeping in spurts through each 24 hour cycle. From everything I've

read, it might be possible to achieve this and eke more hours out of each day and night, but seriously? The experimenters also reported it made them miserable as well as disconnecting them socially from their peers. The juice doesn't sound like it's worth the squeeze on this one.

12. Another alternative is to pretend you're Amish. Go to bed when it gets dark out and rise with the sun. This has the potential to disconnect you socially, as well, of course (unless you're Amish.) Also, if successful, you will awake in the night for a short period. Some wakefulness in the middle of the night is a natural phenomenon that occurs with this kind of sleep cycle.

If your partner shares that cycle, you might spend that time together deep in meaningful conversation or have sex. (You could also have sex if you sleep alone.) This sounds pretty good but, given the demands of readers' lives, I think its widespread adoption is unlikely. It was a very popular lifestyle for a few million years. Then the light bulb was invented, work hours got longer and homework loads got heavier.

13. Remember what Mama said, "No water just before bedtime." If you have to get up to pee once, you've doubled the chances you're going to have to fight the sleep demons.

14. Unclutter your bedroom, clear out the dust bunnies and make sure you are sleeping in a quiet, comfortable haven. Bad news: unless you have a mattress spring poking you in the back, the problem is probably not your mattress. Anti-snore pillows don't seem to work, either.

15. If you're sleepless because of your partner's thrashing or snoring, separate beds or separate rooms may be necessary. I hope that will be a temporary measure.

16. Some proponents of sleep hygiene suggest white noise generators. A continuous low level noise that masks distractions and disturbances may be helpful. However, music meant to lull you to sleep still stimulates the brain. Since the mind is always searching for the new, changes in tones and tunes may keep you awake longer.

17. If you try all of the tactics here that seem reasonable to you and you're still exhausted, suffer insomnia, or have some other sleep disorder, it's time to consult your doctor.

Do the sleep-friendly things.

Lifesaving Tip

Are you snoring a lot? Do you wake up in the night gasping for breath? Has your partner noticed you choking in your sleep? Are you exhausted all the time? Have you ever fallen asleep in an inappropriate situation, like at a stoplight, for instance? If so, ask your doctor for a sleep study to investigate the possibility you have sleep apnea.

Sleep apnea is a dangerous condition. If left untreated, it can lead to serious health problems. Sometimes a dental appliance that brings the jaw forward is helpful and, if you're overweight, your doctors will encourage you to lose the excess pounds and maintain a healthy weight.

The gold standard treatment is a CPAP machine. The CPAP (Continuous Positive Airway Pressure) is a device that keeps your airway open while you are unconscious. It can take some getting used to but, if you need it, it will save your life.

Do the lifesaving thing.

Power Nap Tricks

It's a sad thing, but naps are often reviled, especially by employers. Resistance to your body's signals is one reason drivers fall asleep, kill themselves and/or someone else. We hate the idea that anyone "caught us napping," so much that, if the phone wakes us up, we'll deny we were sleeping.

However, a refreshing nap is one of life's joys. It keeps you sharper when you're ready to get back to work. The key to power napping is to keep it short. Twenty minutes is a good length of time, so set your alarm. You don't want to spoil your night's sleep.

For night owls:

I'm past the age where I think staying up all night is cool. I love that feeling of sleep coming on hard and fast. However, not everyone is on board. We romanticize staying up all night. For coders on deadline, students in emergency cram mode (not recommended) and folks trying to push through an all-nighter for whatever reason, there is a napping trick that's kind of cool. I'm not recommending it and you certainly shouldn't do it often, but I'm not the boss of you.

Here's what you can do to stay sharp after a quick rest:

1. Drink a caffeinated beverage just before you fall into your nap.

2. In about twenty minutes, your body will thank you for the power nap and your brain will be lit up with caffeinated stimulation as the drug (yes, caffeine is a drug) hits your system.

3. Please don't make a habit of this.

If you're a med student enduring the tyrannies of med school shifts, this might get you through grueling and cruel rituals you shouldn't have to endure. For the rest of us, wouldn't it be nice to sleep like a human?

And students — especially high school students — you really need your sleep. Growth spurts and hormonal changes require a lot of rest. Wouldn't it be better not to torture yourself with sleep deprivation? Study incrementally over time to get facts deep into your long-term memory.

**Do the thing that helps you
retain information: sleep.**

Hang Out with the Less Stressed

Despite the daily news, the world really does contain optimistic, stress-resistant individuals. You should seek those people out and hang out with them more.

I have a couple of friends who refuse to see problems. They move on quickly to solutions. They possess an unfailing belief in their ability to deal with whatever stresses may come their way. Most people need a lot of experience to grow their skill and confidence in order to attain this mental state. These individuals seem to have been born confident. Either way, through nature or nurture, get to this happy place.

Maybe my especially confident friends had parents who didn't criticize them too much. Maybe they have a happy chemical imbalance. What I notice about these sorts of people is that their indefatigable optimism is contagious. They're happy. They're successful. They make me want to emulate them.

So why not join them? You are what you pretend to be. Your actions will change your mental state. Gather experience, look at failures as experiments and shrug off the doubters. For any and every endeavor, there are an army of carpers, kibitzers and critics who will tell you something can't be done. But you know what they say about critics. They are the eunuchs at the orgy trying to tell everyone else how to do things right.

Uncomfortable Question Time

1. Do you have negative friends who are constantly putting you down, making you feel bad, draining your energy, adding to your stress or holding you back from your goals?

2. Are you sure those are friends? They sound like enemies.

Since optimists get stuff done, do the friendly thing for yourself and others.

Bonus Uncomfortable Questions

1. Are you the friend who is always negative?

2. If so, why do you think you act that way?

3. What would it look like if you bucked your programming and adopted new, encouraging attitudes?

4. How do you think that would affect your relationships?

5. How would changing your behavior affect your stress levels?

6. Is mean snark making you laugh, but no one else?

7. If anyone were to say the sort of things you say to you, would you get defensive, irritated and hurt?

8. Is negativity really working for you?

9. What leaves the world better than you found it? Snark or encouragement?

10. Are your "harmless jokes" more important than the people you cause stress to?

Do the honest answer thing.

You Change You

Someone once said that the surprise of life is how many lives we live. We live as a child, a young adult, a mature adult. Each phase of you is a different person going through new stages, learning, changing and growing. If negativity is your vice, you can choose to grow out of it.

Negativity can be addictive, maladaptive behavior. Maybe negative behavior is a bad habit that's hurting your career, your relationships and your prospects. Being a jerk isn't much of a stress-free success plan, is it?

I've known several people who try to make a virtue out of a vice. They call themselves delightfully snarky and say, "Hey, this is just me. Take it or leave it." Your smarter friends will take your advice and leave you. That leaves you surrounded by dummies. Ironically, this state of affairs will reinforce your dim view of humankind.

If you have to tell people that you're delightfully snarky in your Twitter profile or in casual conversation, that's a bad sign. That's like announcing your genius. It's powerful if others say it about you but it's just sad if you have to say it of yourself.

If you recognize your negative behaviors reflected in your answers to my questions in the previous chapter, you may be a strain and a drain who spreads stress far and wide. You probably get ignored, blocked and unfriended on social media quite often. And you don't have to live this way.

If you're resistant to this idea and point to professional comedians who make a good living being nasty, I have news for you: that's probably a stage persona. They're playing a character and they aren't that nasty if they aren't being paid.

People *can* change. I knew a guy with a very caustic and hurtful sense of humor. When he realized what he was doing, he changed. He started thinking more before he spoke. He listened more and made new friends. He self-monitored and he simply stopped mistaking nasty for funny.

Stop doing the things that are making you unhappy.

Sentimentality Can Hurt

As I'm finishing up this book for publication, Donald Trump has been elected in the most divisive and nasty election in living memory. It was an ugly campaign. It looks like this is a great time to launch an anti-stress book because everyone on the political spectrum is going to need some stress relief.

Most interesting to me from a stress management perspective was what happened on social media. The division online broke into two camps: I unfollow and block people I disagree with versus friends don't desert friends over political squabbles.

The challenge of social media is that it is designed to feed you what you like. You tend to follow people with whom you agree on Twitter. Facebook notices what you like and gives you more of that while blinding you to other points of view. We're told this is a bad thing, though we make these same alliances in real life, too. We hang out with people who are like us. Much of what we speak and hear bounces around in the echo chamber of our worldview.

For a long time I bought into the idea that listening to other people's point of view is the mature thing to do. I felt that, though I had a couple of old friends with whom I disagreed on several subjects that were close to my heart, I knew these guys in university! I thought I should stick with them for life. I've since changed my mind. I decided that I shouldn't be stuck with anyone for life based solely on inertia, proximity and circumstance.

A healthy exchange of ideas is a good reason to reach across the divide, stay friendly and keep communications going. The trouble is, a lot of what I see in social media is the opposite of a healthy exchange of ideas. It's not mature to stay friends when people are saying things that you consider dumb, hateful, hurtful and relentless. That sounds like needless stress to me.

I guess I thought it was disloyal to abandon old friends just because we disagreed. However, people grow apart. If all you're getting from a relationship is aggravation, what's the point? That's not a friendship. That is a drain.

I am not, of course, suggesting that you dump everyone who disagrees with you. However, if you wouldn't make new friends with someone who espoused the same views, maybe all you've got left with old buddies is the pretense of a friendship.

I'll leave you to think about what you're willing to put up with and draw your conclusions.

Do the thing that makes sense to you.

Forgive Debt

Occasionally, people will end up owing me money. Mostly, it's a relatively small sum and they end up paying eventually. Then there are those who don't pay. They won't. It doesn't matter how much time I give them. Even if I set up a payment plan, they won't pay. It's a write off.

It's a strange and common phenomenon that when you are owed and dare to bring it up, the person who owes you thinks you're a jerk for mentioning it. As long as it's not an amount of money that's worth a small claims action, I *do* write it off.

Usually, my debt forgiveness evaluation happens just before Christmas. The holidays are a nice time to clear off the old worries and welcome the new year. After patient emails have been written and nothing comes of it, I get the deadbeat vibe. I decide whether to pursue the matter further, based on the amount. In most cases, I tell them to forget the debt. Then I forget about it, too. Life is too short to pursue something small and fruitless.

In many cases, forgiving debt is a gift to yourself. The message is not that people suck — though, of course, sometimes they do. My message is that everyone is probably doing the best they can with what they've got and what they know now.

Similarly, if you owe someone money, call them and work out a payment plan. Most people are very reasonable about these things (and they don't relish the conversation any more than you do.) Once you've written a bunch of post-dated checks and sent them off, stop worrying about it. People who make these arrangements to pay off debt are far more impressive to their creditors than those dodging phone calls.

Forgive debt where appropriate. Forgive yourself when you've made your penance. To live, sharks have to move forward. So do we.

Do the shark thing.

Do Not Disturb

My journalism professor in university was a sweet old man beloved by his students. Unfortunately, his office had a door but the walls were windows. Anyone could see him at his desk working away. This sort of setup is an invitation to energy vampires who interrupt coherent thoughts.

When he was on deadline for a magazine piece, a sign would appear on his office door. In angry red marker, the sign read:

I AM *UN-IN*

In other words, "Do not disturb. If you do disturb me, you might be met with small arms fire."

Everyone needs a do not disturb sign. Everyone needs a door to close and a work schedule that family members are aware of and honor. If it's the last Sunday of the month, your teens need to know Mom's working on the bills and filling out her Google Docs spreadsheet. If Mom is bothered, innocent children will be forced to help her.

Protect your space and time. Though many successful businesses have begun at a kitchen table, it's best to have a designated area that is specifically your own. Guard it with troll dolls, harsh words and crime scene tape if you have to.

I also designate work breaks so, when my son wants me to play *Call of Duty* with him, I am available to bond. I'll say, "One more chapter and then I can come up for a couple of rounds." I recharge and we hang out. Then I go back for another round of writing.

When he grabs my shirt and insists I stay to play more video games, I tell him, "If I don't make progress on this book and sell it, how do you plan to pay for college?" That loosens his grip on my shirt.

When my kids were younger, our family did the Daddy daycare thing. My wife went back to work after her maternity leave and I juggled jobs so I could stay home and play with the babies. I still had to work my freelance jobs so, as soon as my wife got home, I tagged out and she tagged in. It wasn't always easy, but we made it work. Even as very young children, the kids respected work time.

How do you buy time when you've got young kids? Here's how I did it:

1. Crowdsourcing. Every week, kids came over to our house. Our kids played with their friends. Sometimes it was just one other child. Sometimes it was several. While I took care of all the kids, their moms and dads did things they had to do. Later the same week, my kids played with their friends elsewhere and I used the time to work.

2. I couldn't afford full-time help but I did manage to find nannies one day a week. It made for a busy day stacking my day like that but the kids had a great time with their caregivers. We mostly recruited university students.

A note about hiring help:

To find good princes and princesses to help you, you may have to kiss some frogs. Interview, get references and don't hire until you can do so with confidence.

3. If family can help, go nuclear. The nuclear family where Grandma and Grandpa are down the block isn't as common as it used to be but, where available and when appropriate, ask for help.

4. Arrange flextime if you can manage it.

5. Get help to get time off, too. The do not disturb sign is a boundary to keep you working efficiently. You can also use it so you nourish your relationships, reconnect with an old friend, nurture your spouse and make time to goof off.

Do the less disturbed thing.

Fix the Small Things

Little irritations add stress to your day that is easily avoidable.

When our shower head acted up, I put off dealing with it for a long time. It still sort of worked but only sort of. It would spray water over the top of the shower curtain if we weren't very careful.

This went on for a while until I finally checked out how much it would cost to have a plumber fix it. It was significantly cheaper to replace the shower head myself. I bought a new, fancier shower head and the problem was fixed in minutes. With a quick Google search or a couple of phone calls, I could have dealt with this quickly and easily. Instead, I let it drag on for a couple of months.

So. That was stupid.

**What simple things need
fixing around your house?
Go take care of that.
Do the things that will make your spouse
think you're useful to have around.**

Bonus for Home Owners

That hinge that's coming loose on that door or cupboard is easily fixed with some white glue and some toothpicks.

YouTube has all sorts of suggestions for common household repairs. Get yourself what you'll need for those repairs: duct tape, a screwdriver set, some washers, fuses, a battery tester, oil, superglue and a hammer and nails. Search up tools and information you need. Get rid of the niggling stresses that suck energy from your days.

Do the handy thing.

Avoid Decision Fatigue

When people name the things that make them feel stressed, they rarely think of decision fatigue. Avoid making rushed decisions on important issues when you're tired. That's one reason why laying out your clothes at the end of the day makes a lot of sense. You may be tired and ready for bed, but you aren't late for work while you're choosing your clothes.

Next step:
dump the propeller beanie.

By that I mean, get rid of the clothes you don't wear. The average man owns approximately 12,000,056 t-shirts by the time he's thirty.* We usually end up wearing the same few favorite shirts and pants over and over. Anything that doesn't fit and anything you don't wear needs to go.

I know you've got something in your closet that you loved in college that reminds you of better days. If it doesn't fit, give it to someone who can use it. Get on with making new and better memories in the days ahead.

Do the thing that helps you find the clothes you want by eliminating the pile the good clothes are hiding in.

*According to an impressive statistic I just made up.

On Clutter

If you've packed something away in a box to gather dust for a year, get rid of it. If it isn't tax records, you can safely do without it.

Maybe you think you live in a small home. Clear out what you don't wear or use. Your home is about to get bigger.

For a refresher on the torment of clutter, see the chapter *The Obstacles at Your Feet*.

Do the thing that adds square footage to your home without having to call in a contractor to knock down a wall.

Accomplish Something Measurable

All times are modern times, but our time more than most produces results that are intangible. Much of our progress is incremental and our products are not concrete. At the end of each day, there is nothing to point to that says, "This is what I did."

It can be easy to fall into the feeling that you are not moving forward and making progress. Over time, it is dispiriting to think that many days it feels like a Sisyphean task. If you feel like you're spinning your wheels, you need some sort of feedback to your brain to let you know that, yes, progress is being made.

Try incorporating tasks into your schedule that signify something tangible. Start each day by making the bed. Do the dishes. Do something that you or someone else can see is a positive change. Weight loss is slow and paperwork never ends, so it's nice to have something to point to.

One of the little pleasures I enjoy is stacking wood for my wood stove. A few cords arrive in the fall and I stack it. It's a good feeling. I build a wall of wood. I'm prepared for a power outage. The furnace could commit suicide during some of the coldest winters on the planet and we'd live. When the wood is stacked and the snow piles up, I get the daily benefit of bringing some indoors to fill the woodbox. To begin and complete a task is a happy thing.

Do tangible things.

A Reminder

I've touched on this topic before, but we're far enough into the book that it's time to remind you of something. This is a confession, to make the point more personal and poignant.

A few years ago, I allowed myself to get sucked into time-wasting controversy way too easily. Whether it was trying to change a bureaucracy or arguing about minutiae on web forums, I was passionate about what I was passionate about. I was a whistleblower. The stakes were pretty low but I let it take up too much space in my head. Worse, in an effort to prove myself right, I argued with idiots who would never change. I wasted my time.

There are good causes and worthwhile fights, but evaluate what battles you join. If the argument is pointless, don't have it. In many corners of the internet, experts and laypeople alike argue over arcane knowledge and nascent research literature. They argue with passion but nothing changes.

A sure sign you're wasting your time is when the participants in any debate aren't actually debating. When know-it-alls fight, you can tell. They aren't sharing any news to help anyone. Their primary concern is showing off, shutting their adversaries up and feeling good about themselves. They provide heat but no light.

When the stakes are low, don't play that game. You have better things to do. You could be sleeping. You could enjoy a book while you soak in a hot bath. In the fall, my favorite exercise is a long walk in the sunshine and crushing dry fallen leaves under my feet. You could be doing just about anything else besides argue and you'll be productive, happy and at peace. When somebody puts up their dukes and says, "Wanna fight?" we can say no.

**Do your equivalent to me crushing
colorful dry leaves on a fresh autumn day.**

A Better Way to Use Your Alarm Clock

When I was a kid, my mother would tell me, "It's time to go up the wooden hill." Meaning: Go to bed! Adults don't usually have moms and dads around to tell them when to go to bed so we stay up too late. Try breaking the habit. Going to bed early truly does feel luxurious.

Don't set an alarm for when you must wake up. Set an alarm for when it's time to wind down and go to bed.

When you set an alarm to go to bed at an earlier hour, you'll probably wake *before* your alarm. Enjoy the hypnagogic state as long as you can.

If you're worried about sleeping in, set another alarm, just in case. I prefer the Sleep Cycle app to an alarm clock. It monitors my movements during sleep so a gentle alarm sounds when I am close to waking anyway. I'm more refreshed that way. However, the morning alarm is only a backup in case I sleep too long. Most days, I wake long before the Sleep Cycle app would wake me.

**Do the alarm thing that
tells you to go to bed.**

A Surprise

As we bring this book in for a landing, I hope you have found at least a few useful tools to better manage your stress. I don't think this book would be complete without an adjustment to your expectations. I want you to get the most out of this book. You've got plenty of questions to ponder, exercises to try and ideas with which to experiment.

However, stress management does take consistent work. It's time to come back to a question from early on. Remember how you rated your stress, pain and energy on a scale of one to ten? You can do that again now. If you have already begun to explore the exercises as I've laid them out, you should find that your stress is lower than it was. (Congratulations!)

If you don't feel like you're making progress, my next question is just as important. If you're ill, injured, in pain or otherwise stressed out, which way are you pointing? Do you feel like you're going to get better at stress management or are things getting worse?

If they're still getting worse, you need to pick up a phone, call a professional and get help. If things are getting better, you may still need to do that. I view these issues holistically. Modern life is so complex, busy and demanding, one solution is rarely the only conclusion. There are many answers for problems at different times in our lives. What may have worked to ease your stress in the past might not work now. No stress is the same.

Be gentle but firm with yourself. If you need to make changes, make those changes consistently and on a daily basis. If the stress management tactics you find are not enough, call in a pro for individual counseling and possibly pharmaceutical interventions. Don't be shy. That's what health care professionals are for.

You need to know that you are not alone in your stress and anxiety. Behind those smiling faces of friends you see on social media are the same worries you have. We are all fragile and searching for love, admiration and approval. We are all searching for connection in some way. Everyone feels stress. We want more. We want to do more. We want to be more. We all worry about the future.

Don't get stressed about stress management. Treat it all as an interesting experiment you're running on yourself. Change may not come immediately but it is my hope that you will have found enough stress management strategies to ease the strain, help yourself and aid others in living a reasonably relaxed and happier life.

You are not alone. Go find someone who feels alone, too. You won't have to go far to find one. If they look like they need it, share this book and join forces in accountability, work your calendars and manage that stress as best as you can.

**Do the loving thing,
for self and other.**

To My Readers

This is my Accountability Commitment with you.

I'm so glad you bought this book. I share and understand your frustrations in dealing with time, energy, stress and pain. In researching this book and writing it, I've improved in many areas. My stress is now low. My pain is mild. My energy is high.

Like many of you, I lived small for too long, too. There are more improvements for me to make. I know that I should start podcasting again. I ran two podcasts but have taken a year off from both of them (the All That Chazz podcast and the Cool People Podcast).

Here's what I need to do personally to align my work life with my dreams to achieve greater success:

1. Podcast more often and regularly. Connect with more readers and listeners.

2. Podcast this book, a chapter at a time, to reach more people and spread the happy word.

3. Connect with thought leaders I've followed and admired for ages, interview them and spread and share their ideas.

4. Write more fiction and non-fiction.

5. Focus on marketing the books I already have.

6. Take the time to go through the webinars I've already purchased to learn how to better market my works.

7. Practice what I preach every day.

8. Enjoy the struggle more, recognizing that no one owes me a living and this is all a journey to experience fully. Greater success comes when I act on what I know without weighing myself down with the burden of entitlement.

9. Overcoming addictions and dealing with challenges is not about New Year's resolutions, made once and soon forgotten. Life management is a daily commitment. Sometimes it's about decisions made on a minute by minute basis.

10. Resentments do not serve me. I'll achieve my dreams when I serve you, my readers, with honesty, integrity and earnest effort.

These are my commitments to myself for the coming year. And you've just been made my accountability partner. You can send me an email to ask me for updates on how my process to success is progressing by emailing me personally at expartepress@gmail.com.

Thank you for reading this book. If you like what you've found here and have discovered something in it that has helped you, I'd appreciate it if you'd leave a review to spread the happy word. (Authors live and die by reviews so please do the happy review thing!)

If you have suggestions for podcast guests or topics you'd like included in future updates or newsletters (or to share your success at life management) please email me at the address above. I read all correspondence from readers and try to respond to everyone when possible.

Now go get out your calendar, write out your next steps to success and stress management. Enjoy the process.

I wish you the very best,

Robert

PS Do the accountability thing with someone. It can be a powerful motivator.

Further Resources

If you're in pain, consider picking up *Pain Free* and *Pain Free for Women*.

These books by physiotherapist Pete Egoscue are genius. He has made the link between posture and pain and suggests series of exercises to help patients get out of pain. His books are written for a lay audience and are useful for anyone looking to remedial exercise for answers to all sorts of somatic problems. By changing our relationship to gravity, stretching, strengthening and promoting bodily symmetry, we can often escape pain.

Becoming a Supple Leopard by Kelly Starrett and Glen Cordoza.

To prevent and rehabilitate injuries, erase stiffness and improve athletic performance, I found this book useful.

Salt, Sugar, Fat by Michael Moss.

Reading how the processed food industry is working to manipulate and addict us might annoy you enough to eat clean. A solid read.

The Four-hour Workweek by Tim Ferriss.

Ferriss became an entrepreneur who joined the "new rich": people who are not necessarily millionaires but who have discovered low-cost living and leveraged their businesses using outsourcing and guile to be more free, to travel and live life on their terms. Check out another of his titles, *The Four-Hour Body*, for compelling reading about cooking, eating well and biohacking.

The End of Heart Disease by Dr. Joel Furhman

I was led to this book by reading Penn Jillette's *Presto!* (referenced earlier in this book). If you're looking for plant-based recipes, this is a good place to start.

How to Stop Worrying and Start Living by Dale Carnegie

This is the stress management classic. If you're looking for more reinforcement for your commitment to live better with less stress, try this one.

Here's a list of podcasts that can help keep you on track:

Dr. Rhonda Patrick, on the *FoundMyFitness* podcast, is a scientist who promotes "strategies to increase healthspan, well-being, cognitive and physical performance." She's a biochemist who really knows her stuff. Highly recommended.

Katy Says with Katy Bowman is a podcast about using movement as nutrition for your health. She delves deep on how to move more to alleviate a variety of health issues.

The 5 A.M. Miracle is a podcast by Jeff Sanders about "dominating your day before breakfast...The core topics include healthy habits, personal development, and rockin' productivity!" If you find your efforts to change your habits are lagging behind your goals, jump in. (Note: despite the title, Jeff is clear that you don't have to rise at 5 a.m. As long as you're up earlier than you normally would be, you can get more done and bust stress, too. Highly recommended.)

The Tim Ferriss Show

This podcast chronicles Tim's interviews with people who deal with stress well, among many other things. Tim is the author of *The Four-hour Workweek* (recommended above). A biohacker, entrepreneur, investor and master communicator, Tim Ferriss finds out how successful people think and explores what they did to become successful.

Rich Roll is the bestselling author and endurance athlete behind the *Rich Roll Podcast*. This is inspirational and informative. Here's the description: "Rich Roll discusses all things wellness with some of the brightest and most forward-thinking minds in health & fitness, including world-class athletes, doctors, nutritionists, trainers, entrepreneurs & artists. Topics include: general fitness & endurance, multisport training, vegan / plant-based nutrition / cooking, meditation, yoga, sustainable lifestyle and beyond. The goal? To help empower you to become your best, most authentic self."

Helpful Gizmos

Lumo Lift

A client recently recommended this device to me. Basically, if you slump, this device will send you gentle vibrations to remind you to adjust your posture. I like shiny ideas and this one seems pretty straightforward: straighten up or get a buzzy reminder. As a big fan of using cues to improve ourselves, I love this idea.

SuperBetter

I first became aware of game designer Jane McGonigle when she spoke at a TedTalk about the devastating concussion that left her in constant pain, unable to work or even speak well. She overcame the effects of her concussion using an app she developed that gamifies the healing process, opening the dopamine pathways in the body's reward system.

Later, I heard an in-depth conversation between Jane and Joe Rogan on his podcast, *The Joe Rogan Experience*. As I write this, I can tell you that I encountered three clients with concussions in the previous two days. The first treatment for concussion that neurologists prescribe is staring at a wall to rest the brain. After your doctor clears you for looking at screens, I recommend SuperBetter.

The news gets even better. SuperBetter is used by people around the world and not just for concussions. It's used by people with all kinds of problems, from recovering from injury to dealing with cancer, heart attack and a plethora of other medical conditions. SuperBetter gets your healing journey pointed in a positive direction.

Fitbit and Garmin

These devices encourage you to move. There are several kinds of these gizmos that measure different variables. The core of movement measurement is to get you to 10,000 steps every day. That which is not measured doesn't change, so if your aim is to move more, try them. If you're just curious how much you move at present, get a cheap pedometer to find out what your daily baseline is.

SleepCycle

I use this app every night. I occasionally suffer insomnia but not nearly as often as I did before SleepCycle. Instead of a regular alarm clock setting, the app monitors your movement in bed and wakes you within a range of time when you are close to waking anyway. I'm more prone to rising refreshed that way.

If I don't wake before the alarm is set to go off, it wakes me gently. My song, Bobby Caldwell's *What You Won't Do For Love*, starts off low and slowly gets louder. That's a better way to start the day. I also find that the device's measurement of my movement in the night is surprisingly accurate and the graphs are fascinating. Check it out.

Food trackers

There are many electronic food trackers you can try. I like the apps myfitnesspal for activity tracking and Out of Milk for planning my grocery list. The Weight Watchers app is also very useful.

Email management systems

Inbox Pause makes your emails arrive in batches. You set the number of times per day the influx arrives. Boomerang allows you to delay the sending of messages so you can clear your inbox without having to give someone an immediate reply. With these tools, you run your email instead of allowing it to run you.

The School of Life by author and philosopher Alain de Botton.

This is one of my favorite YouTube channels. Devoted to "emotional education," you're going to love these insightful and thought-provoking videos.

Other Titles You May Enjoy
The author also writes fiction under the name Robert Chazz Chute.
Get the latest titles at AllThatChazz.com.

Science Fiction

The Robot Planet Series
Machines Dream of Metal Gods
Robots Versus Humans
Metal Immortal
Metal Forever
and the *Robot Planet Omnibus*

Wallflower
(A Time Travel Novel)

Dark Fantasy

This Plague of Days Series
Books One, Two and Three
and the *This Plague of Days Omnibus*

The Dimension War Series

Haunting Lessons
Death Lessons
Fierce Lessons
Dream's Dark Flight

Crime Fiction

Brooklyn in the Mean Time

The Hit Man Series (Coming in 2017)

New York Punch
Chicago Kick
Hollywood Hook
Bronx Choke
Chinatown Chill

Coming of Age/Literary (Coming in 2017)

Bright Lights, Big Deal

Anthologies

Self-help for Stoners
Murders Among Dead Trees

Non-fiction

Crack the Indie Author Code

Learn more at AllThatChazz.com.

About the Author

Robert Chute graduated from the University of King's College with an honors degree in Journalism and a minor in Philosophy. He became a Registered Massage Therapist in 1993. He lives in Canada with his wife and children and has written more than twenty books.

To find out more about Robert's fiction or listen to his stress relief podcast, visit AllThatChazz.com.

To schedule an appointment or to order signed paperbacks of this book, visit MassageTherapyScience.com.

www.ingramcontent.com/pod-product-compliance
Lightning Source LLC
Chambersburg PA
CBHW031125090426
42738CB00008B/974